Los Angeles Daily News

ON TOP OF THE WORLD

THE LOS ANGELES DODGERS' EXTRAORDINARY RUN TO THE 2024 WORLD SERIES TITLE

This book is available in quantity at special discounts for your group or organization. For further information, contact:

Triumph Books LLC
814 North Franklin Street
Chicago, Illinois 60610
Phone: (312) 337-0747
www.triumphbooks.com

Printed in U.S.A.
ISBN: 978-1-63727-844-4

Content packaged by Mojo Media, Inc.
Joe Funk: Editor
Jason Hinman: Creative Director

Southern California News Group
Ron Hasse, President & Publisher
Frank Pine, Executive Editor
Tom Moore, Executive Sports Editor
Caroline Wong, Sr. Director of Marketing
Julie Corlette, Marketing Manager
Michele Cardon and Dean Musgrove, Photo Editors

Front Cover Photo by Los Angeles Daily News: Keith Birmingham
Back Cover Photo by AP Images

AP Images

Contents

Introduction

By Bill Plunkett | October 30, 2024

Has any team ever won so much and received so little credit for it?

They have made the playoffs 12 consecutive years with five 100-win seasons and an average of 98.7 wins per full season. They have 11 division titles in those 12 years, annually running off with the National League West.

But critics 'only' want to talk about what they didn't do.

Coming into this postseason, they had only won one World Series title in those years, during the pandemic-shortened 2020 season when they only played 60 games before heading into a bubble.

Never mind that there is an organization-wide belief that they had another World Series stolen from them (by the sign-stealing Houston Astros of 2017). Never mind that they played under the same rules as every other MLB team in 2020 and emerged from the longest and most uniquely challenging postseason in baseball history.

"I'm going to take the high road," Dodgers manager Dave Roberts said of the criticism after the Dodgers put all that behind them with an unequivocal, dominant run to their first full-season World Series title since 1988.

The best team in baseball (98-64) during the regular season, the Dodgers ran through the San Diego Padres, the New York Mets and, finally, the New York Yankees in the postseason and needed just five games to beat the Yankees and claim the eighth championship in franchise history.

It was no more than what was expected of the Dodgers in 2024.

Their annually high expectations only grew during a 10-day stretch of December 2023 when they committed over $1 billion to new players – including a record 10-year, $700 million deal that brought two-time MVP Shohei Ohtani to Los Angeles.

Outsized as they were, Ohtani managed to exceed expectations in his first year with the Dodgers (even though he won't resume pitching until 2025). Drawing fans and marketing opportunities unlike any other baseball player (and few professional athletes ever) along the way, Ohtani had the first 50-50 season in baseball history – 54 home runs and 59 stolen bases – assuring he will be named the National League's Most Valuable Player.

It will be his third MVP award, the first ever won by a player who spent his season primarily as a DH. He will be only the second player in MLB history to win MVP awards in both leagues (joining Frank Robinson).

But it wasn't that easy for the team.

The Dodgers' path to the postseason was lined with potholes that had them swerving all over the road. Twelve different starting pitchers spent time on the injured list. Only three (four if you include rookie Landon Knack who did not start in the postseason) made it to October healthy – Jack Flaherty (acquired at the trade deadline), Yoshinobu Yamamoto and Walker Buehler. Mookie Betts missed two months with a broken hand. Max Muncy missed three with a rib injury. Freddie Freeman had the most challenging season of his career, dealing with his young son's illness off the field, a broken finger and severely sprained ankle on the field.

It didn't matter. The bullpen stepped up and bullpen games became the omnipresent pumpkin spice of the postseason that Dodger fans learned to like. Freeman played on with one good leg.

"We did not have 'easy' in our playbook all year," Dodgers president of baseball operations Andrew

Boyle Heights artist Robert Vargas' Shohei Ohtani mural titled "LA Rising" adorns the side of the Miyako Hotel on First Street in Los Angeles. (Los Angeles Daily News: Keith Birmingham)

Friedman said. "This is as challenging a season in terms of the injuries and adversity and things that popped up as I can remember."

The postseason run started with its own challenge. The Padres won two of the first three in the Division Series, raising the specter of another first-round failure. But the Dodgers won the final two games to take the DS, spinning a postseason record-tying 33 consecutive scoreless innings out of an 'it-takes-a-village' approach to getting outs.

The streak spilled into the NL Championship Series where the Dodgers dispatched the New York Mets in six games, setting up the matchup everyone craved – none more than the FOX Network or MLB's marketing execs.

The 12th World Series meeting between baseball's bi-coastal elite, the Dodgers and Yankees, was their first since 1981. But it came with the added star power of the sport's two biggest names – Ohtani and Aaron Judge.

Neither Ohtani nor Judge were big factors in the series. Instead, Freeman homered in each of the first four games, drove in a postseason-record tying 12 runs and will be remembered forever for his Kirk Gibson moment in Game 1 against the Yankees.

It was a season Dodger fans will relive for years to come.

Bill Plunkett is the Dodgers beat writer for the Los Angeles Daily News, Orange County Register *and the Southern California News Group.* ■

WORLD SERIES GAME 1
October 25, 2024 | Los Angeles, California
DODGERS 6, YANKEES 3 (F/10)

Iconic

Freddie Freeman's Walk-Off Grand Slam Sends Dodgers Past Yankees in World Series Opener

By Bill Plunkett

For 36 years, the Dodgers have been waiting for their next Kirk Gibson moment. They might have just gotten it.

Hobbled by a sprained ankle throughout this postseason, Freeman put an exclamation mark on a Game 1 that packed enough drama to fill an entire seven-game series. His walk-off grand slam with two outs in the 10th inning lifted the Dodgers to a 6-3 come-from-behind victory over the New York Yankees on Friday night.

It was the first walk-off grand slam in World Series history. Only two players have hit a walk-off home run while trailing with two outs in a World Series game – Gibson in Game 1 of the 1988 World Series and Freeman in Game 1 of the 2024 World Series.

"I played the whole game, though," Freeman said of the comparisons.

Gibson's iconic homer came in a pinch-hit appearance, his only at-bat of that World Series.

"I'm probably one of, like, two people in here that was alive when that happened," 37-year-old reliever Daniel Hudson said.

"It was almost the same situation, obviously. Bottom of the ninth, Game 1 of the World Series, a lefty comes up and absolutely nukes one. The comparisons between the two are just really freaking cool. Just to be a part of it was awesome."

The Yankees were on the verge of taking the early advantage in the best-of-seven series after left fielder Alex Verdugo made a spectacular catch of Shohei Ohtani's foul fly for the second out of the 10th inning. After the Yankees intentionally walked Mookie Betts to load the bases, Freeman jumped on the first pitch he saw from left-hander Nestor Cortes and lined it into the right field seats.

"When you're five years old with your two older brothers and you're playing wiffle ball in the backyard, those are the scenarios you dream about – two outs, bases loaded in a World Series game," Freeman said, describing the feeling as he rounded the bases as "floating."

"For it to actually happen and get a home run and walk it off to give us a 1-0 lead (in the series) – that's as good as it gets right there."

Freeman raised his bat high as the sellout crowd of 52,394 exploded, making the ground rumble and the stands rock.

"Might be the greatest baseball moment I've ever witnessed, and I've witnessed some great ones," Dodgers manager Dave Roberts marveled. "I cannot believe what just happened. That's what makes the Fall Classic a classic, right, because the stars come out and superstars make big plays, get big hits, in the biggest of moments. … I'm speechless right now."

Freddie Freeman launches a game-winning grand slam that will go down as one of the most memorable moments in franchise history. (Los Angeles Daily News: Keith Birmingham)

It was the most dramatic ending to a World Series game at Dodger Stadium since Max Muncy's walk-off home run in the 18th inning of Game 3 in 2018, the longest game in World Series history.

"When I hit mine you kind of black out in that moment. So I don't remember a lot from that moment," Muncy said. "This one I was able to see a lot more what went on – the reactions, you feel the ground shaking, the fans, the teammates.

"I was actually standing on the top step (of the dugout), talking to Doc and I was holding my bat and saying, 'There's actually no way I can get up this inning. I don't know why I have my bat.' I was going to go on deck because you have to help the guy if there's a passed ball or something. So I was just standing there thinking, 'Why am I holding my bat?' As soon as he hit it, I just launched my bat."

The Yankees will try to even the series on Saturday in Game 2. Yoshinobu Yamamoto is scheduled to start for the Dodgers against Yankees left-hander Carlos Rodón.

"We can't sit here and mope," Yankees slugger Aaron Judge said. "Learn from it, where we can improve, and try to win the next one."

Just when we all thought dominant starting pitching in the postseason had gone the way of dodo birds, eight-track tapes and affordable housing – up popped a pitchers' duel between Gerrit Cole and Jack Flaherty.

Cole gave up a two-out triple to Freeman in the first inning. Alex Verdugo misplayed the carom off the wall in foul territory, allowing the gimpy-legged (but rested) Freeman to get all the way to third.

"This last week has been really good for me," Freeman said. "The first time I ran was when I ran out to give high fives to my teammates when we got introduced (before the game)."

Cole retired Teoscar Hernandez to strand Freeman – and 10 more Dodgers in a row after that. Kiké Hernandez broke the string when he lined his own triple into the right-field corner in the fifth inning. This time, Will Smith lined a sacrifice fly to right field, Hernandez tagging and just beating the throw home with a head-first slide for the first run of this World Series.

Flaherty was coming off a troublesome start in Game 5 of the National League Championship Series when he gave up eight runs and lasted just three innings. His fastball velocity was back up and he held the Yankees scoreless through five innings.

Juan Soto led off the sixth inning with a single. Flaherty struck out presumptive American League MVP Judge for the third time in the game.

That brought up Giancarlo Stanton, who looked bad as he swung and missed at two low breaking balls. After Flaherty misfired with a high fastball, he went to the well one more time. Stanton golfed that one high into the air 412 feet down the left field line and over the Dodgers' bullpen for a two-run home run.

It was Stanton's 17th career postseason home run, sixth this postseason (he was the ALCS MVP) including one in each of the past four games. It held up as the difference in the game until the eighth inning.

Shohei Ohtani lined a double off the right field wall that missed going over by just a couple feet in the eighth inning. The Yankees misplayed the relay throw, a critical mistake that allowed Ohtani to go to third base. He trotted home from there when Mookie Betts flew out to center field, tying the score.

More drama awaited at the left field wall.

With two outs in the ninth, Gleyber Torres hit a long fly ball to the wall in left that a fan reached over and snatched. Ruled fan interference, Torres was stopped at second base. Roberts put his head in the lion's mouth – intentionally walking Soto to bring up Judge – and pulled it out when Blake Treinen got Judge to pop out.

Treinen struck out Stanton to start the 10th inning but gave up a single to Jazz Chisholm who stole second against Treinen's slow-developing motion. The Dodgers intentionally walked Anthony Rizzo and Chisholm stole third.

With the infield in, Anthony Volpe hit a grounder up the middle that Edman dove and smothered. But he could

Teoscar Hernandez and Freddie Freeman are all smiles after the dramatic comeback win in Game 1 of the World Series. (Los Angeles Daily News: Keith Birmingham)

only shovel the ball to Lux at second base for a force out as the deciding run scored.

A walk and a single put the tying and winning runs on base for Ohtani with one out in the 10th. But Verdugo made his running catch, tumbling into the stands. That allowed the runners to move up and prompted the Yankees to walk Betts.

"Just taking the left-on-left matchup there. No, I didn't deliberate long," said Yankees manager Aaron Boone, who brought in Cortes to face Ohtani. Cortes was a starter all season until a flexor strain sent him to the injured list in September. He was not on the Yankees' playoff roster until the World Series.

"The reality is he's been throwing the ball really well the last few weeks as he's gotten ready for this. I knew with one out there, it would be tough to double up Shohei if (another lefty reliever) Tim Hill gets him on the ground and then Mookie behind him is a tough matchup there. So I felt convicted with Nestor in that spot."

Freeman jumped on a first-pitch fastball and lined it at 109.2 mph off the bat. The rest was history.

"One of the most, if not the most incredible game I've ever been a part of," said Chris Taylor, on base for Freeman's slam as a pinch-runner. "You couldn't have written a better ending. Freddie's been through a lot, this whole season but this whole postseason as well, battling through injury. For him to be the guy to come up in that big spot, it was perfect." ∎

For El Toro

Dodgers, Fans Honor Legacy of Fernando Valenzuela Before Game 1 of World Series

By Todd Harmonson | October 25, 2024

On an October Friday in Dodger Stadium, just shy of his 21st birthday, Fernando Valenzuela delighted a full house when he gutted his way through a rough outing to beat the New York Yankees and reverse the course of the 1981 World Series.

Whether the fans were the 12-year-old Mexican American kid next to his dad in the top row of the reserved level in seats they were selected to buy in a postcard drawing or the longtime season ticket holders far closer to the action, they were enthralled throughout what turned out to be the final start of Valenzuela's spectacular rookie season.

On an October Friday 43 years (and two days) later, fans gathered again to pay tribute and say goodbye to one of the most beloved Dodgers before, appropriately, Game 1 of the 2024 World Series against the New York Yankees. Valenzuela died Tuesday at 63 years old after an illness that his family has kept private.

The Dodgers honored Valenzuela with video and musical tributes – the latter a rousing Spanish-language performance by Deyra Barrera and Julian Torres – before the players were introduced, and then they took the tribute up a notch.

Valenzuela's former Dodgers teammates Orel Hershiser and Steve Yeager, both wearing Valenzuela jerseys, brought out the ball for the ceremonial first pitch. Instead of throwing it, though, they placed it near the blue No. 34 painted on the mound.

Then Valenzuela's wife, Linda, and children joined the Dodgers on the baseline for a moment of silence that eventually gave way to a chant of "Toro, Toro" from the early arriving fans.

Juan Carlos Gonzalez from Eastvale was one of the many who made the trek well ahead of the first pitch. He didn't want to miss the tribute and made sure to get a picture of Valenzuela's No. 34 at the top deck level entrance to Dodger Stadium among the team's other retired numbers.

"Fernando was a great representative of our Mexican heritage and was a huge part of why people loved the Dodgers for a long time," said Gonzalez, who at 43 said he was too young to see Valenzuela play but still understands why he was revered in Los Angeles.

Gonzalez said it was important enough to be at Game 1 with his son, Andre, for the tribute to Valenzuela that he bought tickets on the secondary market late Friday morning.

"It wasn't cheap, but it's worth it," he said.

Linda Avila from Gardena showed up Friday in the No. 34 jersey she's owned for 10 years and wore to each Dodgers playoff game since the team announced that Valenzuela had been hospitalized.

Her husband Nacho remembered attending the Dodgers' home opener in Valenzuela's rookie season – a last-minute start in place of injured teammate Jerry Reuss – when Avila bought 80 tickets for friends and family to join in the fun.

"So many great memories," said Nacho Avila, a longtime season ticket holder. "It's great to be here on a day they're honoring him."

Dodgers legends Steve Yeager, left, and Orel Hershiser place a ball on the mound in honor of Fernando Valenzuela before Game 1 of the World Series. (AP Images)

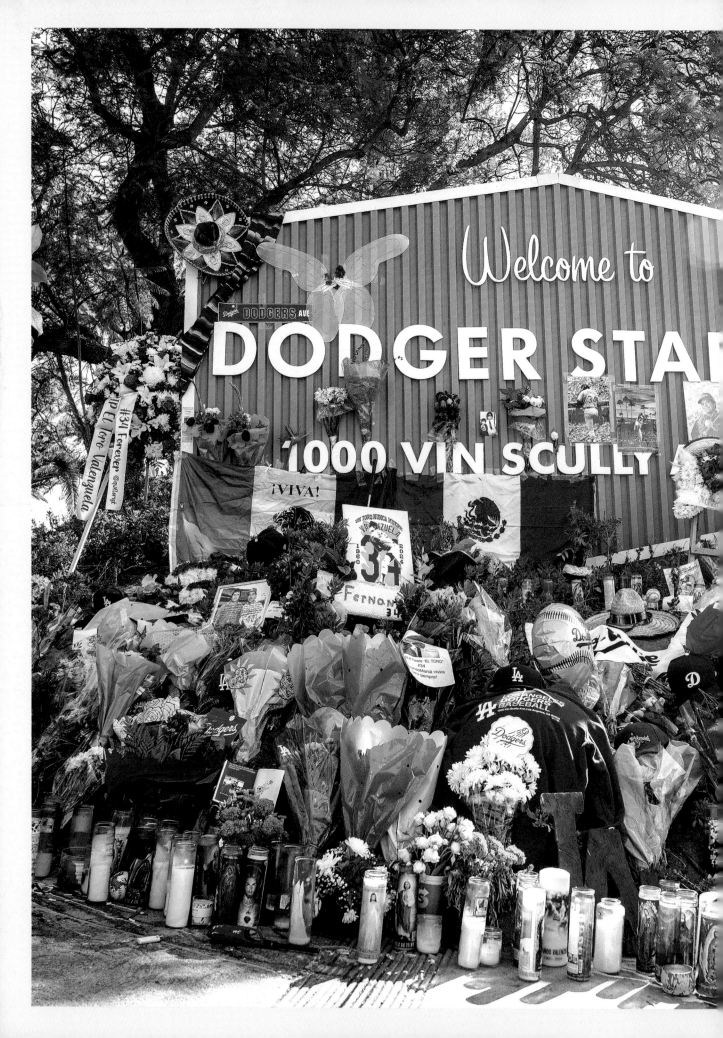

The path to Dodger Stadium was easy to follow Friday. One No. 34 jersey after another showed the way, starting in the line for taquitos at Olvera Street's Cielito Lindo and stopping briefly at the Dodger Stadium sign on Vin Scully Avenue, where the first flowers were placed within an hour of the Dodgers' announcement of Valenzuela's death. The memorial on Friday included funeral sprays, balloons, Mexican flags, photos and messages to a local hero.

The path of No. 34 jerseys picked up again from the parking lots to the admission gates. One of the security guards at the top deck level said he was going to fist-bump everyone who was wearing a Valenzuela jersey, and he stayed busy in the first 30 minutes that fans streamed into the stadium.

Eddie Alaniz of Corona sported a twist on the traditional white jersey with blue letters; his was the red, white and green of the Mexican flag.

"I first saw Fernando when he was a reliever at the end of the 1980 season," Alaniz said. "We didn't know anything about him at that point, but he was amazing. I was always a fan."

Sergio Castro from Lake Elsinore walked up to Valenzuela's retired number and placed flowers on the growing tribute.

"He played baseball the way it's supposed to be played," said Castro, who took a picture of his son, Anthony, by the No. 34. "It never seemed to be about the money. It was because he loved it."

Castro said he knew the ideal way for the Dodgers to honor Valenzuela.

"Beating the Yankees in the World Series would be perfect," he said. ∎

The tributes to Fernando Valenzuela were heartfelt and wide ranging, as the franchise icon was memorialized by fans leading up to what would turn out to be an unforgettable World Series opener. (Los Angeles Daily News: Sarah Reingewirtz)

WORLD SERIES GAME 2
October 26, 2024 | Los Angeles, California
DODGERS 4, YANKEES 2

On the Same Page

Dodgers Ride High After Freddie Freeman's Fireworks, Grab 2-0 World Series Lead

By Mirjam Swanson

About the whole "whole new ballgame" thing. What if that's a whole bunch of baloney? Because if you're the Dodgers and Freddie Freeman has, only hours before, set off an impromptu firework show across L.A. with his historic blast in the 10th inning to win Game 1 of the World Series, no, you don't try to immediately turn the page.

Why would you want to?

All you want to do is keep the good times going. And so the Dodgers have, chasing Game 1's dramatics with a 4-2 victory in Game 2, jumping ahead 4-1 on Saturday night and holding off the New York Yankees after that at Dodger Stadium.

The Dodgers now need only two more victories as the best-of-seven World Series heads to New York, with Games 3, 4 and, possibly, 5, set for Monday, Tuesday and potentially Wednesday.

It was, as Ice Cube – the rapper and Saturday's pregame opening act, would tell us – a couple of good days in L.A.

Would have been all good if the Dodgers' global superstar Shohei Ohtani hadn't hurt his left shoulder sliding into second base in the seventh inning Saturday.

Seeing their biggest star walk off the field cradling his arm took some wind out of the Dodgers' sails, but still, a steady wind is still at their backs heading east.

The first two victories of this series will, of course, be remembered most for Freeman's grand slam off of New York Yankees left-hander Nestor Cortes on Friday night – the first walk-off grand slam in World Series history, and the kind of thing you wear for a bit after experiencing it.

Either as a badge of honor or as a bruise.

One of those where-were-you-when sports moments, an all-timer that went down as just the third walk-off home run in postseason history by a player whose club was trailing, à la Joe Carter in 1993 and Kirk Gibson's iconic shot for the Dodgers in '88.

The type of thing that, depending on your perspective, had you going to bed either in a state of bliss or fury, and waking up the same way.

And when you're on the right side of a spectacle like that, it's probably not hard to convince yourself that it's fate knocking: After all, it's been documented that Gibson's homer had landed at 8:38 p.m., and that Freeman's cleared the wall at 8:39 p.m.

"We celebrated the heck out of last night, as I thought we should have," said Dodgers manager Dave Roberts, who acknowledged Saturday was "a new day" but "I do think there's some kind of momentum, excitement that will carry over to (Saturday's) game."

So, no, Dodgers shortstop Miguel Rojas told me Saturday morning – with Friday's roaring crowd still echoing in all of our consciousness, he didn't plan to flush that feeling. He wanted to ride it. Relish it. Add some mustard.

Freddie Freeman went deep for the second consecutive game, this time helping the Dodgers take a commanding 4-1 lead in the third inning. (Los Angeles Daily News: Keith Birmingham)

"We use that as a momentum and as a confidence booster," said the Dodgers' veteran, who returned to the lineup after being left off the Dodgers' National League Championship Series roster with an adductor injury.

"Knowing that we're down to the last out ... knowing that you walk one guy to face another Hall of Famer is really good on our side."

The Yankees have future Hall of Famers on their team, too, of course. But those guys had to absorb Freddie's Friday gut punch, and they were left reeling, pressing and guilty – especially in presumptive American League MVP Aaron Judge's case – of over-reaching for pitches.

So far this series, Judge has gone 1 for 9 with six strikeouts, including swinging and whiffing six times in his four at-bats. For the postseason, he's 6 for 40 with two homers and 19 strikeouts.

And without his help, the Yankees mustered only four hits Saturday – and only against starter Yoshinobu Yamamoto – though they did load the bases with one out in the top of the ninth inning.

The Dodgers, meanwhile, added some Ice Cube to their cup running over with good vibes and proceeded to hit Yankees starter Carlos Rodón as if they were batting around beach balls, tagging him with six of their eight hits and all four of their runs in 3⅓ innings.

"You definitely do need to ride some emotions, but you also have to understand that each day is a new day," Dodgers outfielder Mookie Betts said after he went 2 for 4 with a run Saturday, extending the playoff success that eluded him in recent years. "You need to enjoy it, but you also have to understand there's business to take care of."

Or as reliever Alex Vesia put it after he came on to record the final out, getting Jose Trevino to fly out: "It's not always gonna go our way. But one pitch at a time, one out at a time, Dodgers all the way." ■

Teoscar Hernandez broke a 1-1 tie with his two-run home run in the third inning with what would prove to be the decisive runs in the Game 2 win. (Los Angeles Daily News: Keith Birmingham)

WORLD SERIES GAME 3
October 28, 2024 | New York, New York
DODGERS 4, YANKEES 2

'We're Right There'

Freddie Freeman Homers Again, Dodgers Stifle Yankees for 3-0 World Series Lead

By Bill Plunkett

Rapper Fat Joe sang before Game 3 of the World Series on Monday night at Yankee Stadium.

The fat lady could be up next.

The Dodgers got a two-run home run from Freddie Freeman in the first inning and never looked back, moving within one game of their first full-season championship since 1988 with a 4-2 victory over the New York Yankees.

Starting with Freeman's 10th-inning walk-off grand slam in Game 1, the Dodgers have outscored the Yankees 12-4 while taking the first three games of this Series. They will go for the championship – and the first World Series sweep since 2012 (San Francisco Giants over Detroit Tigers) – in Game 4 on Tuesday night at Yankee Stadium. It would be only the second sweep in the 12 World Series meetings between these two rivals (the Dodgers also did it in 1963).

"Just really focusing on winning the game tomorrow as a team," Dodgers star Shohei Ohtani said through his interpreter. "There's nothing better than to be able to have the opportunity to do so."

Ohtani has replaced Freeman as the wounded Dodger heroically playing on. Ohtani emerged for pregame introductions wearing a brace or heating pad on his injured left shoulder under his jacket and clutched his left arm close to his body when running the bases. He went 0 for 3 but reached base twice – on a walk and when he was hit in the foot by a pitch.

Freeman, meanwhile, has clearly recovered from the sprained ankle that hampered him so badly during the first two rounds of the postseason. He turned on an inside cutter from Yankees starter Clarke Schmidt in the first inning Monday night and lined it into the right-field seats for a two-run home run.

"Just based off what he's done the last three games – we obviously have to find a way to win one more game, but let's say we win one more game at some point – I expect Freddie to never pay for a meal ever again in L.A.," utility man Kiké Hernandez said.

Freeman also homered in the third inning of Game 2, making him only the third player to homer in each of the first three games in a World Series (Barry Bonds in 2002, Hank Bauer in 1958). Freeman also homered for the Atlanta Braves in Games 5 and 6 of the 2021 World Series, giving him home runs in a record-tying five consecutive World Series Games. George Springer also did it for the Houston Astros in the 2017 and 2019 World Series.

"This game is hard – round ball and round bat, and moving a lot of different ways and coming fast," Freeman said. "So I'm thankful that it (his swing) is in a good spot right now when we need it the most.

"I'm just seeing the ball very well. I'm swinging at the strikes, taking the balls. It's what you're trying to do every game. And thankfully, I've been able to do that."

In perhaps his final game in a Dodgers uniform – he will be a free agent this winter – Walker Buehler recalled

The Dodgers' Freddie Freeman, right, watches his two-run home run along with Yankees catcher Jose Trevino during the first inning in Game 3 of the World Series. (AP Images)

his own history. Pitching like the Buehler of old, he held the Yankees scoreless for five innings, allowing just two hits and two walks.

"Listen, man, we play professional baseball for a living," Buehler said. "When it's going good, there's not much else you'd rather do on this earth."

There were few times during the regular season when Buehler had that feeling. But his 5.38 ERA from the regular season has been irrelevant in the postseason. Buehler allowed six runs in the second inning of Game 3 in the National League Division Series against the San Diego Padres – then gave the Dodgers 12 consecutive scoreless innings through the rest of his postseason. He has allowed just one run in his 18 career World Series innings.

"We all knew what he was going to do. We all know he turns into a different animal in the postseason," reliever Anthony Banda said.

"It's just in his DNA," second baseman Gavin Lux said. "Some guys just have it. … The bigger the moment the bigger they perform. Walker's got that in him. He always has. You just see that different look in his eyes. The bigger the game we all want Walker out there."

That six-run inning in the NLDS was fueled by poor defense – so they owed him one. The only time Buehler ran into trouble against the Yankees, the defense stepped up around him.

Giancarlo Stanton doubled with one out in the fourth inning (the first hit off Buehler). Mookie Betts made a diving catch on Jazz Chisholm's sinking liner for the second out before Anthony Volpe dropped a single into left field. Teoscar Hernandez came up throwing, firing a 93.9 mph bullet (his fastest throw of the season via Statcast) on one hop to catcher Will Smith who tagged Stanton out to keep the Yankees scoreless.

"The Teo throw was huge. It obviously killed the momentum," Dodgers manager Dave Roberts said. "Mookie's play on the sinking liner from Jazz. … I thought Walker was kind of feeling it a little bit. There was starting to be a bit more hard contact. So to make a defensive play on a sinking liner and then the play at home plate was huge for all of us."

After the power burst by Freeman, the Dodgers took more pedestrian routes to tacking on single runs in the third and sixth.

In the third, Tommy Edman drew a leadoff walk, went to second on Ohtani's ground out and raced home on Betts' bloop single to right field. In the sixth, Gavin Lux was hit by a pitch, stole second and just beat the throw home to score on Kiké Hernandez's single to center field.

Roberts made his bullpen calls with one eye on Tuesday's pitching plan – and continued to make all the right choices, as he has throughout this postseason run.

But he had to survive scares in the sixth and seventh innings. Most dangerously, the Yankees put two runners on with two outs in the seventh. With Juan Soto on deck, Anthony Banda struck out Gleyber Torres when home plate umpire Mark Carlson called a 2-and-2 fastball that was clearly above the zone strike three.

"I'm not answering that," Banda said when asked if the pitch really was a strike.

The Dodgers were one out away from their fifth shutout of this postseason (which would have tied Cleveland's postseason record from 2016) when Alex Verdugo hit a two-run home run off of Michael Kopech.

"I think for some of the guys that were here – Kiké, Clayton (Kershaw), the coaches, Austin Barnes, I think Blake Treinen, just some guys that were here with us – we want that parade," Roberts said, referring to the Dodgers' last World Series championship, won on a neutral field following the pandemic-shortened 2020 season. "We never got a chance to celebrate with the city of Los Angeles. That's something of an incentive.

"But outside of that, you have an opportunity to be a world champion. So we're right there." ■

Designated hitter Shohei Ohtani rounds the bases on a two-run home run by Freddie Freeman. Ohtani grabs the neckline of his jersey to stabilize his left shoulder, which he injured two days prior. (AP Images)

WORLD SERIES GAME 4
October 29, 2024 | New York, New York
YANKEES 11, DODGERS 4

Bombs Away

Yankees Hit 3 Home Runs in Game 4 to Postpone Dodgers' World Series Party

By Bill Plunkett

From the franchise that brought you, "It ain't over 'til it's over" – it ain't.

With Anthony Volpe's third-inning grand slam providing shock treatment, the New York Yankees lurched to life with an 11-4 victory over the Dodgers in Game 4 of the World Series.

After being outhomered 5-2 in the first three games of the best-of-seven series, the Bronx Bombers (the major-league leaders in home runs during the regular season) hit three in Game 4.

"They're gonna fight," Dodgers outfielder Mookie Betts said of the Yankees. "If you made it this far, you have a resilience in you. You're gonna fight the whole time. We expected that. Obviously we didn't play well today, and they did. And that's why they won."

Even the Yankees fans had more fight in them in Game 4. Betts reached into the stands in foul territory to catch Gleyber Torres' first-inning fly ball and two fans tried to rip the glove off his hand. Fan interference was called and both fans were ejected from the game.

"We lost. It's irrelevant," Betts said when asked about the play. "I'm fine. He's fine. Everything's cool. We lost the game, and that's what I'm focused on. We gotta turn the page and get ready for tomorrow."

The Yankees' first win of the Series prevented the first World Series sweep since 2012 (San Francisco Giants over Detroit Tigers) and forced a Game 5 at Yankee Stadium. Game 1 starting pitchers Jack Flaherty and Gerrit Cole return to the mound.

The Dodgers tried to close out the Series with a bullpen game in Game 4. It was a collective flop and the Dodgers essentially spent the second half of the game in punt formation, saving their high-leverage relievers.

"I don't think anyone expected those guys to lay down. We had some at-bats that I thought could have been better, but we knew it was a bullpen game," Dodgers manager Dave Roberts said. "As far as outcomes, to have six guys in your 'pen that are feeling good, rested, I feel good about that."

Freddie Freeman dropped a cone of silence on Yankee Stadium with another first-inning home run, a two-run line drive into the comfortably-close right field seats. It was the fourth consecutive game in the series and his record-setting sixth consecutive World Series game with a home run (dating to Games 5 and 6 with Atlanta in 2021).

The Yankees got one of the runs back in the second inning as Ben Casparius navigated his first major-league start as a World Series opener. He walked three of the first seven batters he faced and gave up a double off the wall to Austin Wells with Volpe at second. Volpe danced around off second base as Betts pursued the drive and somehow didn't score on the play. He did make it home on a ground out to cut the Dodgers' lead in half.

Veteran Daniel Hudson got the third-inning assignment. He struck out Juan Soto to start the inning but lost his way after that.

He hit Aaron Judge with a pitch, gave up a single

off the wall to Jazz Chisholm Jr. and walked Giancarlo Stanton to load the bases. After Anthony Rizzo popped out, Volpe came up with just one hit and seven strikeouts in his first 12 at-bats in this World Series. He got a first-pitch slider at the knees from Hudson and lined it into the left field seats for the sixth grand slam across MLB this postseason, a new record, that electrified the crowd.

"I just couldn't stop the snowball from getting bigger," Hudson said. "Couldn't make a pitch. Thought I made to a pitch to get Rizzo right there. Just threw a really bad slider. Just kind of one of those that just pops out of your hand and you have that instant, 'Oh no' feeling in your stomach."

The Dodgers started chipping away at the Yankees' first lead since the 10th inning of Game 1. Will Smith led off the fifth inning with a home run. Tommy Edman drew a walk and went to second when Shohei Ohtani dumped a single into center field.

Betts bounced into a force out to put runners at the corners. Freeman hit another ground ball to second baseman Gleyber Torres, who flipped high to Volpe to start a double play. But Freeman had hustled down the line on his bad ankle and replays showed he beat the throw at first base, allowing a run to score.

It was Freeman's franchise-record 10th RBI of this Series and made him only the seventh player in World Series history with 10 or more RBIs (the first in the National League). He is the first to do it in just four games at the start of a Series.

"I probably would've laughed," Freeman said when asked if he could have envisioned having this kind of Series a few weeks ago when his ankle was at its worst.

"I'm telling you, we really got out of the woods on that. Obviously it's still swollen, but I feel good, I'm in a good spot. You saw me flying down the line. I feel good and I have no concerns about it right now."

The Yankees tacked on with a solo home run by Wells off Landon Knack in the sixth inning then broke it open with a five-run eighth inning against Brent Honeywell Jr., including a three-run home run by Torres and – perhaps more ominously – an RBI single by Judge

(now 2 for 15 in the World Series).

"That was sick," Wells said of the charge Volpe's grand slam put in the team. "When he hit that ball, I knew it was hard off the bat and we were going to score some runs. Then it went over the wall, and I was like … that felt a little bit like when Judgey hit the grand slam off the Red Sox earlier in the year."

The Yankees had scored just seven runs in the first three games. They got their first seven RBIs in Game 4 from the bottom three hitters in their batting order (Volpe, Wells and Verdugo), who had entered 4 for 32 with three RBIs in the Series.

"Honestly, I feel like it really just takes one big swing, and I feel like that was Volpe's big swing there," Wells said.

"I think also the situation we were in – I think that we just kind of needed to say screw it and go after it and have fun because some guys may never come back to the World Series again. So enjoying the game, and I think that allowed us to play a lot looser tonight."

The Yankees' Game 4 breakout didn't surprise Freeman.

"I think we're gonna be okay," he said with a smile. "This team knows what we have to do tomorrow. We knew they were going to come out and we weren't gonna keep those bats down very long. They came out swinging. We'll try to do the same thing tomorrow." ∎

WORLD SERIES GAME 5
October 30, 2024 | New York, New York
DODGERS 7, YANKEES 6

Start Spreading the News!

Dodgers Storm Back from 5-Run Deficit to Win First Full-Season World Series Title Since 1988

By Bill Plunkett

For all their sophisticated analytical brainpower, there is one set of numbers the Dodgers had not been able to make add up.

One short-season title in 11 seasons.

But the math has been re-set. The Dodgers fought back from a five-run deficit and beat the New York Yankees, 7-6, in Game 5 on Wednesday night, taking the eighth World Series in franchise history, the first since that 'bubble' title in 2020 and – say it with me – their first full-season championship since 1988.

"Now it's two, baby. Now it's two," third baseman Max Muncy said in the celebratory clubhouse, acknowledging that the criticism "absolutely" stung the Dodgers' core group. "What are you going to say now?"

So many special moments were lost to the pandemic in 2020 – birthdays, weddings, graduations. The Dodgers reclaimed theirs – specifically the nine players from that team who participated in this year's World Series. They will get their parade.

"This is No. 2 for us. The first one was just as much as this, in my opinion. People can say what they want, but this was No. 2 for us. Hopefully we get a few more," Dodgers catcher Will Smith said.

"We've been wanting a parade since 2020. We couldn't do it because of the circumstances, but I can't wait to celebrate with our fans, the best fans in baseball."

In Dodgers lore, it will be remembered as a heroic comeback – the largest comeback ever in a World Series-clinching victory – in Game 5, closed out by Walker Buehler cementing his big-game credentials. But it was one of the most horrendous defensive innings in World Series history that brought them back.

Unable to put the New York Yankees away with a bullpen game in Game 4 on Tuesday night and unwilling to go for a potential knockout blow by deploying their best relievers in a losing game (albeit one with a one-run margin in the middle innings), the Dodgers gave the Yankees the gift of life Tuesday night.

Held to just three home runs in the first three games, the major-league leaders in longballs hit three in Game 4 and three more in the first three innings of Game 5.

Dodgers starter Jack Flaherty has been both good and bad, alternately, during this postseason. The bad version showed up Wednesday night.

He walked the second batter he faced, Juan Soto, then gave up back-to-back home runs to Aaron Judge

Freddie Freeman hoists the Willie Mays World Series Most Valuable Player trophy after Game 5. Freeman homered in the series' first four games, and tied the World Series record with 12 RBIs. (AP Images)

and Jazz Chisholm Jr. Flaherty gave up a leadoff double in the second inning and an RBI single to Alex Verdugo and Dodgers manager Dave Roberts brought out the Yu Darvish hook – the one that is both quick and too late at the same time. Darvish lasted just 10 batters in Game 7 of the 2017 World Series but five of them scored and the Dodgers couldn't recover.

Roberts has said multiple times this year that the difference between this year's Dodgers team and those previous teams that fell short of the ultimate goal was their willingness to fight.

Down 5-0 without a hit through four innings against Yankees ace Gerrit Cole, they fought.

"This game was no different than our entire season," Muncy said. "Get dealt a couple blows, come back from it. Get dealt some more blows, come back from it. This game was literally our season in a nutshell."

Tommy Edman led off the fifth inning with a single. Then the bungling began.

Judge made a spectacular catch at the wall in the fourth inning, but he flubbed a line drive right at him for an error. Will Smith hit a ground ball to shortstop Anthony Volpe. He had the lead runner at third base but made a poor throw into the dirt and everyone was safe.

With the bases loaded and no outs, Cole struck out Gavin Lux and Shohei Ohtani and Mookie Betts dribbled a ball to first baseman Anthony Rizzo. The inning should have been over.

But Cole had stopped running to cover first base and could only watch helplessly as Rizzo, playing back, was too slow to beat the hustling Betts. The Dodgers' first run scored, and the inning went on.

"After they scored three in the first, every half inning we came in, we were like 'Just get one. Chip away, chip away,'" first baseman Freddie Freeman said. "Obviously we didn't do that the first couple of innings. In this game, when you're given extra outs, you've got to capitalize. That's what we were able to do in that fifth inning."

Freeman drove in two with a single to center field. His 12 RBIs in five games tied the World Series record (Bobby

Richardson of the Yankees in the seven-game 1960 Series) and earned him the World Series MVP trophy.

Teoscar Hernandez followed with a drive to the wall in center field for a two-run double to tie the score. All five runs in the inning came after there were two outs – and should have been four.

"We just take advantage of every mistake they made in that inning," Hernández said. "We put some good at-bats together. We put the ball in play."

But Brusdar Graterol walked three in the sixth inning and the Yankees regained the lead on a sacrifice fly.

But the Dodgers still had some fight in them. A broken-bat single by Kiké Hernandez and an infield single by Tommy Edman started the eighth-inning comeback. Mix in a walk, a catcher's interference and two sacrifice flies and the Dodgers emerged leading for the first time in the game.

Flaherty's early exit turned Game 5 into yet another bullpen game and Roberts had another night of antacid moments.

"We've got to give Doc his flowers tonight," Freeman said later. "An inning and a third (from the starter) – he covered that whole game and our bullpen was incredible."

Bullpen and their plus-one.

Roberts trusted Blake Treinen to shut down the Yankees in the sixth inning then rode him through the seventh and eighth innings.

Judge doubled off Treinen with one out in the eighth and Chisholm walked. Manager Dave Roberts walked to the mound with Treinen at 37 pitches.

"I looked in his eyes. I said how you feeling? How much more you got?" Roberts recalled. "He said: 'I want it.' I trust him."

Treinen retired Stanton on a flyout and his 42nd pitch struck out Anthony Rizzo with two runners on to end the eighth.

It was an heroic effort – but Roberts needed another hero to get him three more outs. On came Game 3 starter Buehler, who would have been throwing his between-

The Dodgers were jubilant on the field at Yankee Stadium after recording the final out in Game 5 to secure the franchise's eighth World Series crown. (AP Images)

starts bullpen session in preparation for a Game 7 start.

Instead, he retired the side in order in the ninth for his first major league save and the Dodgers celebrated on the field at Yankee Stadium.

"There were 30 other guys on this team that would have taken that inning," Buehler said. "I was just in the right spot."

Playing with an injured shoulder after Game 2, Shohei Ohtani – the $700 million man who set so much of this year's story in motion – was just 2 for 19 in his first World Series with no RBIs and just 14 for 61 (.230) in his first postseason.

But he filled in the only blank on his baseball resumé and was at the center of the post-game celebration, hoisting the trophy as if he had two good arms and spraying champagne with abandon.

"I think there is a legitimate argument that he is the greatest player to ever play this game," Dodgers president of baseball operations Andrew Friedman said. "Obviously all this does is help further that.

"Seeing him tonight, celebrating, he said, 'Alright, nine more!' In his first year, we won a championship, so he thinks this is easy. We'll just do this nine more times." ∎

Undeniable

Dodgers Cement Their Status as Baseball's Best

By Jim Alexander | October 30, 2024

It figured, didn't it?

An improbable season, one in which the Dodgers achieved the best record in baseball even as their injured list expanded, ended in an improbable victory on Wednesday night in the Big Apple.

Before now, according to the people who look these things up for Fox Sports, no team had come back from a five-run deficit to win a World Series clincher. And by the end of the second inning of Game 5, the Dodgers were staring at a 5-0 deficit, starter Jack Flaherty was done for the evening after facing just nine batters, and Yoshinobu Yamamoto was probably already gearing himself up mentally to pitch a Game 6 against the Yankees on Friday night at Dodger Stadium.

Stand down, Yoshinobu. Your next obligation will be Friday, all right, but it's going to be a parade through the streets of L.A.

Yes, the Dodgers are World Series champions. And maybe you can describe them as champions of the world, a team with representatives from Japan, Cuba, Venezuela, the Dominican Republic and Puerto Rico. (Kiké Hernández literally wrapped himself in the Puerto Rican flag during the on-field celebration.) And, if you want to take World Baseball Classic representation into account you can add Canada, even though Freddie Freeman was born and grew up in Orange County.

They got here even while using 40 pitchers over the course of the season, while having two full starting rotations worth of hurlers on the injured list, and while losing Max Muncy and Mookie Betts to injury for significant periods during the season, having Freeman hobbled by an ankle injury for the first two postseason series and Shohei Ohtani nursing a partially dislocated shoulder in the final three games of this one.

(This, after Ohtani – supposedly distracted with the investigation into the gambling activities, and ultimate embezzlement, involving former interpreter Ippei Mizuhara that surfaced during the opening series in Seoul – ignored said distraction and had one of the greatest individual seasons in baseball history, becoming the charter member of the 50-50 club.)

In a sense, this championship story was improbable because of recent history, two straight first-round losses turning the fan base a bit gun-shy and a thin starting pitching rotation also dampening expectations.

As it turned out, one of those starters, Walker Buehler, channeled his inner Orel Hershiser and closed out the ninth inning Wednesday, with the Dodgers having used all of their leverage relievers, to preserve the 7-6 victory in Yankee Stadium that finished this World Series in five games.

What was it that the late Vin Scully said, after a

Mookie Betts pumps his fist after hitting a sacrifice fly in the eighth inning of Game 5, driving in Tommy Edman for what would prove to be the game-winning run (AP Images)

home run out of nowhere in 1988 started the Dodgers toward what was their last full-season championship before this? "In a year that was so improbable, the impossible has happened."

Can we suggest that maybe there is an unseen hand that guides these things? In '88, Game 1 was decided by the hobbled Kirk Gibson's walk-off home run, his only at-bat of the World Series, and the Dodgers beat the mighty Oakland A's in five games. In '24, Game 1 was decided by Freeman's 10th-inning walk-off grand slam, and while it's not an exact comparison it was a similar lightning bolt, as anyone in the stadium for both home runs can attest.

And yes, the Dodgers beat the Yankees in five games, and maybe in retrospect that Game 1 finish had a deflating effect as well.

One other similarity between the two full-season titles: In '88 the Dodgers were running out of position players because of injuries, and there was an urgency to clinch the World Series in five before anybody else got hurt. In '24 a pitching staff seemingly held together by chewing gum and baling wire somehow made it to the end. It wasn't always pretty, and there were times in the postseason – including Tuesday night's Game 4 – when Manager Dave Roberts had to marshal his resources, opting to sacrifice the present in pursuit of the main goal.

It worked.

But while you can count the improbables, these Dodgers really are baseball's best team, and you couldn't make that case in '88 until the very end. This team finished the regular season with the game's best record. They fought off elimination in the first round against San Diego – which, as it turns out, was the toughest team they faced in the postseason and very easily could stake a claim as the second-best team in baseball (but, sorry, Padre fans, you get no parade).

Then they swept through New York, eliminating the Mets in six and the Yankees in five.

"There's a number of fingerprints all over this win," Dodgers president of baseball operations Andrew Friedman said during the postgame on-field ceremony. "Scouting department, player development … there's a number of people. It's a special group."

Game 5 displayed some of the reasons why these Dodgers are the best team in the game. They're relentless offensively, and they took full advantage every time the Yankees opened the door. Two errors and a failure by Yankees starter Gerrit Cole to cover first base on Betts' grounder to the right side contributed to the five-run fifth inning that tied the game, and a catcher's interference call aided the two-run eighth that wiped out a 6-5 Yankees lead and decided the game.

And when closing time arrived, after Blake Treinen – the last leverage guy Roberts had at his disposal – gave him 2⅓ innings, Buehler pitched a 1-2-3 ninth, punctuating the night by striking out former teammate Alex Verdugo.

"Seventh inning, he just said that he's going to be available," Roberts said. "I didn't … see that even coming to play, but obviously as the game sort of played on, we had to keep the game close. Our guys were fighting, so I just felt that at that point in time, I was going to be all in."

Maybe the things that happened along the way – starting in the opening series in Seoul with the Mizuhara revelations – hardened these players' spines and contributed to a cohesion that made all of this possible.

"I think sometimes when those things kind of happen, it just rallies a group of guys together," said Freeman, who was named the World Series MVP. "When you start supporting a teammate in his first year, like we did, for (Ohtani) to go out there and have the greatest season, I think, of all time, (it was) pretty special.

"It seems like we hit every speed bump possible over the course of this year. And to overcome what we did as a group of guys, it's special. This is what we start out to do every single spring training, to win a championship. I think it's the hardest thing to do in sports because you just never know what's going to happen. I mean, we were down 2-1 in the NLDS and it easily could have gotten

Dodgers President & CEO Stan Kasten holds up the Commissioner's Trophy during the celebration following the clinching Game 5 win in New York. (AP Images)

away from us. And to come back and win those two games and keep it going like we did, it's just a special group of guys."

Roberts noted, in his pregame briefing Wednesday night, that this was an unusually cohesive team, and "when you're around people you care about, that you believe in, you're just better collectively."

Afterward, he elaborated.

"We did go through a lot, but I'll say we still had the best record in all of baseball this year," he said. "It wasn't easy, but our guys fought and played every day the right way, played to win.

"There was a lot of backfilling on talent because of injury. A lot of young players cut their teeth, which is good. But one thing is that we just kept going. Even in the postseason, I don't think anyone had us picked … to get out of the first series. For us to go out there and fight and scratch and claw and win 11 games in October, that's a credit to our guys."

And yes, there will be that long-awaited parade on Friday. Maybe they can invite some of the guys from the 2020 – and even 1988 – champs to join them. ∎

THE 2024 SEASON

Billion-Dollar Flex

Dodgers Head to Spring Training in 'Full Villain Mode'

By Bill Plunkett | February 7, 2024

Don't hate them because they're rich.

The Dodgers have used their financial muscles annually since the Guggenheim Group took over ownership, carrying one of – and frequently – the highest payrolls in baseball each season.

But this winter's billion-dollar flex took things to another level.

The Dodgers have done the 'super team' thing before. But they open spring training this week having bought and paid for (or put on layaway to pay later) the best free agents available this winter – domestic (Shohei Ohtani) and international (Yoshinobu Yamamoto) – and one of the best players to change teams via trade (Tyler Glasnow), adding in a few extras (Teoscar Hernandez and James Paxton) along the way.

This spending spree was not universally cheered.

"There's just something about those guys that you don't like. Can't explain it," San Francisco Giant ace Logan Webb said after the Dodgers' binge. "It kind of added to that.

"Giants players, we all texted each other. We didn't like it."

Former Dodgers right-hander Ross Stripling started the winter as one of those Giants players before a trade to the Oakland A's. On a podcast, he said the Dodgers had crossed a line with this winter's moves.

"The way I look at it is that they are just going full villain mode in a way," Stripling said. "They've always had the payroll. But they've done an unbelievable job in drafting and developing talent. I think that World Series team (in 2020) had, like, 16 homegrown Dodgers on it. Now, it's Freddie. It's Mookie. It's Shohei and Yamamoto and they're coming for everybody."

Stripling is not wrong.

Of the 27 players who appeared in the 2020 World Series for the Dodgers, 13 of them were homegrown products. The roster most likely to break camp and head for the season-opening games in South Korea this spring could have as few as five homegrown Dodgers on it with only three – Will Smith, James Outman and Gavin Lux – likely to be in a starting lineup dominated by high-dollar imports like Ohtani, Betts and Freeman.

But if anyone doesn't like the way the Dodgers spent their money – too bad, Betts said.

"If you've got it, then you can, you know?" he said. "You do things that other people can't do. That's what makes you good, right? That's what makes people better than the next guy, because he can put out more power than the next guy. He can do this better than the next guy.

"Somebody's bankroll may be a little bit longer. There's nothing you can do about it. ... They used it. Sorry."

Betts' economic philosophy is endorsed by his teammates.

"I think Mookie said it best – what do you want us to do?" third baseman Max Muncy said. "We're trying to win. We're assembling a good team. ... If people want to call us the villains, that's fine. It doesn't change who we are in the clubhouse. It doesn't change who we are to our

The Dodgers signed two-way star Shohei Ohtani to a staggering 10-year, $700 million deal. Ohtani would serve as the Dodgers' designated hitter while recovering from an elbow injury that kept him off the mound. (Los Angeles Daily News: David Crane)

fans. It doesn't change who we are in the stadium. We've got to go out there and perform."

Shortstop Gavin Lux dismissed any criticism that what the Dodgers did this winter was "bad for baseball."

"I don't see how. I think Mookie said it the best – how can you not go out there and try to get the best players possible?" Lux said. "Twenty-nine other teams could have done it. So I don't see how it could be bad for baseball if everybody else could have done it. Like Mookie said, what do you expect us to not try to get the best guys to win? Our goal is to win a World Series so of course we're going to go get the best guys out there. I don't know why you wouldn't do that."

The Dodgers have won a lot over the past 11 seasons – an average of 99 wins in the 10 full seasons (including 100 or more in each of the past four) and 10 division titles. But they have just one short-season championship to show for it – a championship devalued in some eyes – and back-to-back first-round playoff failures the past two Octobers.

This winter's spending spree is already seen in some quarters as an attempt to correct that by buying another championship.

"Believe me, I wish buying a championship meant we win a championship," Freeman said. "But I think anyone in this game knows how hard it is to win a championship. I'm just glad our ownership gave us a chance to do it. That's really all you can ask for as players. To give us the best chance to win a World Series this year and many, many more beyond, that's your ultimate goal."

This winter's acquisitions are not short-term investments. Ohtani signed for 10 years, Yamamoto for 12, Glasnow for five.

Ohtani was asked what the Dodgers have to do now to make those investments be seen as wise.

"I mean, the only choice is winning the World Series," Ohtani said through his interpreter.

Mookie Betts defended the Dodgers' offseason spending spree, which included Yoshinobu Yamamoto, Tyler Glasnow and Teoscar Hernandez, in addition to Shohei Ohtani. (Los Angeles Daily News: David Crane)

Yoshi's World

Dodgers' New Starter Tackling Challenges of New League, New Team

By Bill Plunkett | February 11, 2024

Shohei Ohtani is a known commodity, a six-year MLB veteran with a Rookie of the Year, two MVP awards and a host of honors for his two-way prowess.

But the Dodgers' other big signing this offseason is more of a mystery. Right-hander Yoshinobu Yamamoto is the highest-paid pitcher in baseball history, signed to a 12-year, $325 million contract before he has even thrown a pitch in the major leagues.

"Certainly I don't think anyone expected this coming into the offseason," Dodgers manager Dave Roberts said of the massive contract it took to land Yamamoto. "I think it's just part of timing. It's part of demand. I think it just lined up perfect for both of us.

"We've had eyes on him for years. Now with the metrics and things like that, the way his body moves and the four pitches that he has and commands, betting on the guy and the person – all that stuff makes us feel really confident in the investment. … We saw a player that we really wanted."

The player they are now seeing in camp for the first time does not fit the usual profile of an elite starting pitcher. For one thing, the 25-year-old Yamamoto is listed at 5-foot-10 – but appears smaller when standing with the rest of the Dodgers' pitchers. No other pitcher on the Dodgers' 40-man roster is listed under six feet tall and Yamamoto's likely rotation-mates to start the season are 6-foot-8 (Tyler Glasnow), 6-foot-5 (Bobby Miller), 6-foot-4 (James Paxton) and 6-foot-5 (Emmet Sheehan).

"Everybody is bigger than me," Yamamoto acknowledged with a smile through his interpreter Sunday.

Yamamoto stands out from the crowd for his unique routine as well – starting with throwing a javelin to build arm strength.

"Obviously a lot of players already know about it," Yamamoto said. "I'm getting a lot of attention for that."

His workouts focus on mobility and flexibility, eschewing weight training. The routine has allowed him to generate a fastball that approaches 100 mph despite his stature and stuff that Gavin Lux deemed "nasty" when he stood in the batter's box during Yamamoto's bullpen session on Friday.

"The one thing about Yoshi is he does things kind of different," Roberts said. "The javelin is something he feels comfortable with as far as the prep work of getting him ready to throw. It's certainly worked. I think there's going to be a lot of things that he does that we haven't done here that we might learn from him too.

"I don't think he touches a weight. …. When you see him he's not a very physical guy. But he's got a lot of body control, body awareness."

The results in Japan couldn't have been better. Yamamoto comes to MLB off three consecutive MVP seasons and three consecutive Sawamura awards (the Japanese league's equivalent to the Cy Young), giving the Dodgers confidence that he can make the jump.

"He's got a really good foundation as a jumping off point," Dodgers president of baseball operations Andrew Friedman said. "He's incredibly talented. The arm talent is very unique. His ability to command the baseball is very unique."

But there are also those unknowns.

Yoshinobu Yamamoto agreed to a 12-year, $325 million contract with the Dodgers following a decorated career in Japan with the Orix Buffaloes. (Los Angeles Daily News: Keith Birmingham)

Yamamoto pitched once a week in Japan. Though the Dodgers will monitor his workload carefully in his rookie season, the right-hander will pitch more frequently than he has in his life. And the ball used in MLB is slightly different than what Yamamoto has been throwing in Japan.

"I don't have the experience throwing on shorter rest," Yamamoto said. "But I did everything I could do in preparation – adjusting mechanics, and a lot of different other things. So I will keep adjusting as needed."

While Ohtani has had six seasons to acclimate to life in the United States, Yamamoto is making those adjustments for the first time. Veteran Miguel Rojas did what he could to make both Yamamoto and Ohtani feel at home in their new clubhouse.

"I know what it's like to come from a different country, join a new team," Rojas said. "So I wanted to do something to make them feel welcome."

Yamamoto and Ohtani found bottles of wine in their lockers following Sunday's workout, courtesy of Rojas – cabernet sauvignon from Quintessa as recommended by Freddie Freeman, Rojas said.

Yamamoto posted a photo of the wine on his Instagram account along with the note Rojas attached — "Welcome to the family. I'm super excited to be ur teammate and play behind you!!!"

"The vibe of the team and the clubhouse is amazing," Yamamoto said. "That makes it easier for me to focus on what I need to do." ∎

Strong Opening in Seoul

3 Singles, 2 Walks and a Broken Glove Lead to a 4-run 8th Inning and a 5-2 Victory

By Bill Plunkett | March 21, 2024

The people of Seoul welcomed Major League Baseball with open arms, pounding drums, dance teams and coordinated cheering. The Dodgers welcomed the San Diego Padres to the slow water torture their lineup could inflict on opposing pitching staffs this season.

Seven hits and nine walks – four of them involving pitch-clock violations by the Padres' pitchers – kept turning that lineup over until the Dodgers broke through for four runs in the eighth inning to beat the Padres, 5-2, in their season-opening game Wednesday.

"I just think there's no give," said Gavin Lux, who inadvertently pushed across the go-ahead run in his first regular-season game since 2022. "One through nine, everyone's going to give you a tough at-bat. We're going to grind you down, grind you out and plus you've got guys that can do damage up and down the lineup, too.

"Today was a good look at. We're not going to give up, not going to give in and one through nine, we're going to grind you down."

The most anticipated season perhaps in Dodgers franchise history started in historic fashion for its location, 6,000 miles from Los Angeles in Seoul's Gocheok Sky Dome, and the trifecta of former MVPs at the top of their lineup – Mookie Betts (2018 American League), Shohei Ohtani (2021 and 2023 American League) and Freddie Freeman (2020 NL).

It was only the fourth time in major-league history a team had former MVPs batting 1-2-3 in their lineup – the Cincinnati Reds did it in 1976 (Pete Rose, Joe Morgan and Johnny Bench) and again in 1978 (Rose, Morgan and George Foster) and the Philadelphia Phillies in 1983 (Rose, Morgan and Mike Schmidt).

The Dodgers' trio did what they could to light a fire through seven innings. Betts and Ohtani were on base twice each and Freeman three times. But the Dodgers went a collective 0 for 7 with runners in scoring position before they broke through in the eighth with Betts and Ohtani each stroking RBI singles.

"The biggest thing is that we got that W and the way we got it, coming back late in the game like that proves that we're a really good team," Shohei Ohtani said through his interpreter after going 2 for 4 with a stolen base and an RBI in his Dodgers debut.

Ohtani got his first hit as a Dodger with two outs in the third inning, ripping a high fly ball foul down the right field line (with an exit velocity of 119.2 mph) then ripping a single to right two pitches later (112.3 mph off the bat).

"Sometimes with hitters, one swing gets you back," Dodgers manager Dave Roberts said. "And even in spring, he was getting some hits. But I really feel that one swing where he pulled it in the air foul, he really took a good swing and I think that bled into that at-bat where he lined a ball into right field for a hit and had another big base hit later in the game."

Ohtani's new wife, Mamiko, had barely stopped sharing high-fives in the Dodgers' family seats when her husband stole second base on the next pitch. Back-to-

As part of the MLB World Tour program, the Los Angeles Dodgers and San Diego Padres met for two games at the Gocheok Sky Dome in Seoul, South Korea. The Seoul Series also marked the regular-season debut of new Dodger Shohei Ohtani. (AP Images)

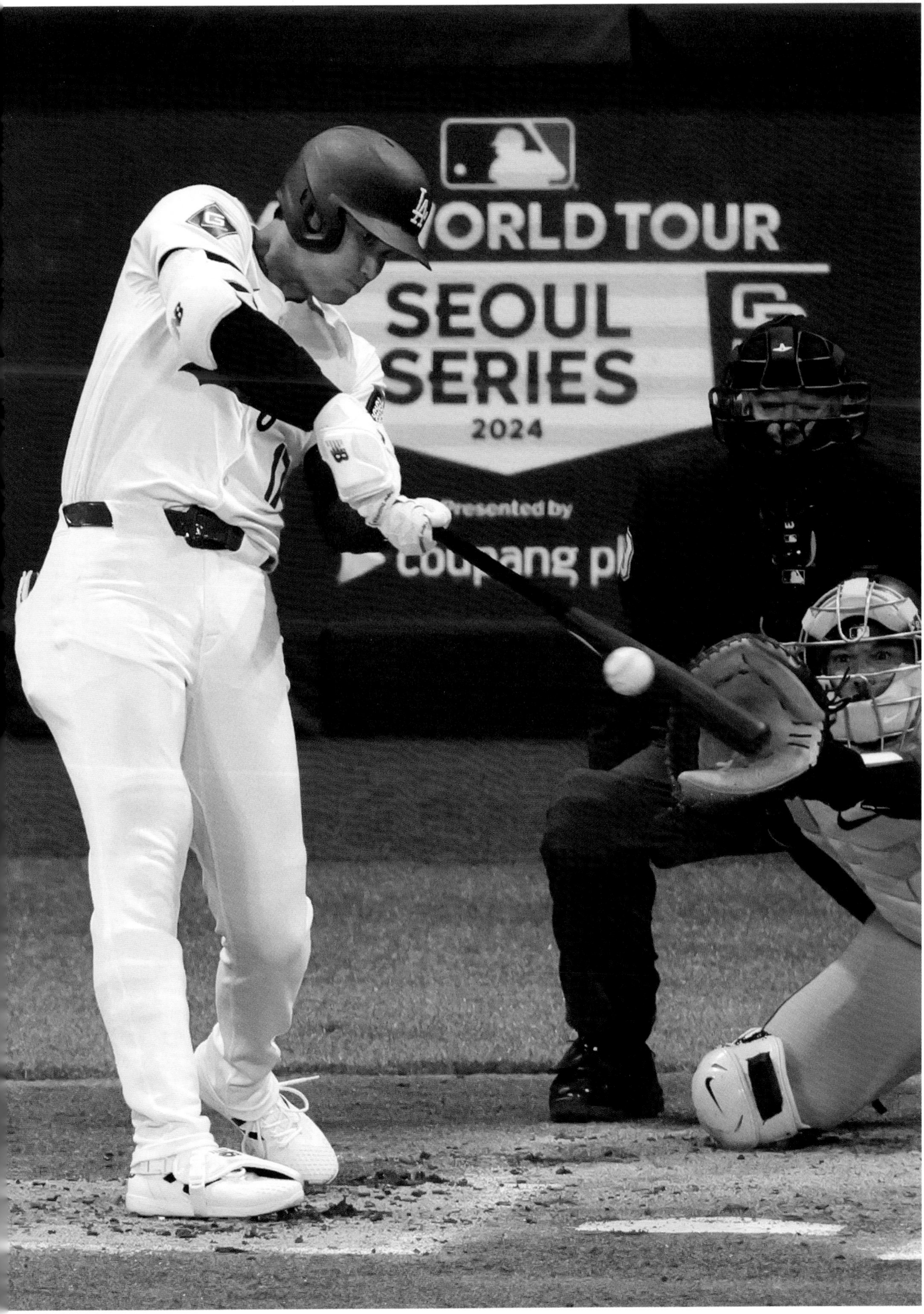
WORLD TOUR
SEOUL
SERIES
2024

back walks – eight Padres pitchers combined to issue nine walks and hit one batter – loaded the bases for Max Muncy but he struck out.

An inning later, an error by third baseman Tyler Wade allowed Teoscar Hernandez to reach base and he eventually scored the Dodgers' first run of the season on a sacrifice fly by Jason Heyward. But the Dodgers went into the eighth, down 2-1.

"I felt like we could have scored a lot more runs if I'd gotten on earlier or gotten on after Mookie," Ohtani said. "I think there were a lot of chances to score more runs than we did today."

They finally broke through in the eighth – literally.

Two walks and a single loaded the bases with no outs. Kiké Hernandez tied the game with a sacrifice fly before Lux rolled over and bounced a ground ball to the right side of the infield.

First baseman Jake Cronenworth got to it and appeared set for a 3-6-1 double play, but the ball broke the webbing of his glove and bounced through for an error on a rare "equipment failure" call, the go-ahead run scoring on the play.

"I didn't realize it broke through his web – I thought it just ticked off, and then I saw him run back to the dugout, like, 'What the (heck)?'" Lux said. "I'll take being lucky right there, I guess."

Betts and Ohtani followed with RBI singles.

"It sucks," Cronenworth said of the costly play. "I don't know what else to say."

The Padres did little offensively, managing just four hits in the game despite Tyler Glasnow being far from sharp in his five innings. Glasnow bounced numerous curveballs and walked four, giving up single runs in the third and fourth innings – both set up by leadoff walks.

"It was bad. The whole game, I just didn't have it," he said of the curveball. "Honestly, just my slider today is kind of what I was pitching off of. And then everything else felt kind of inconsistent. I tried to get it back later. But it was just one of those days where it was not really there." ■

Ohtani celebrates after scoring on a double by Will Smith during the Dodgers' season opener. Ohtani went 2 for 4 with a stolen base and an RBI in his Dodgers debut. (AP Images)

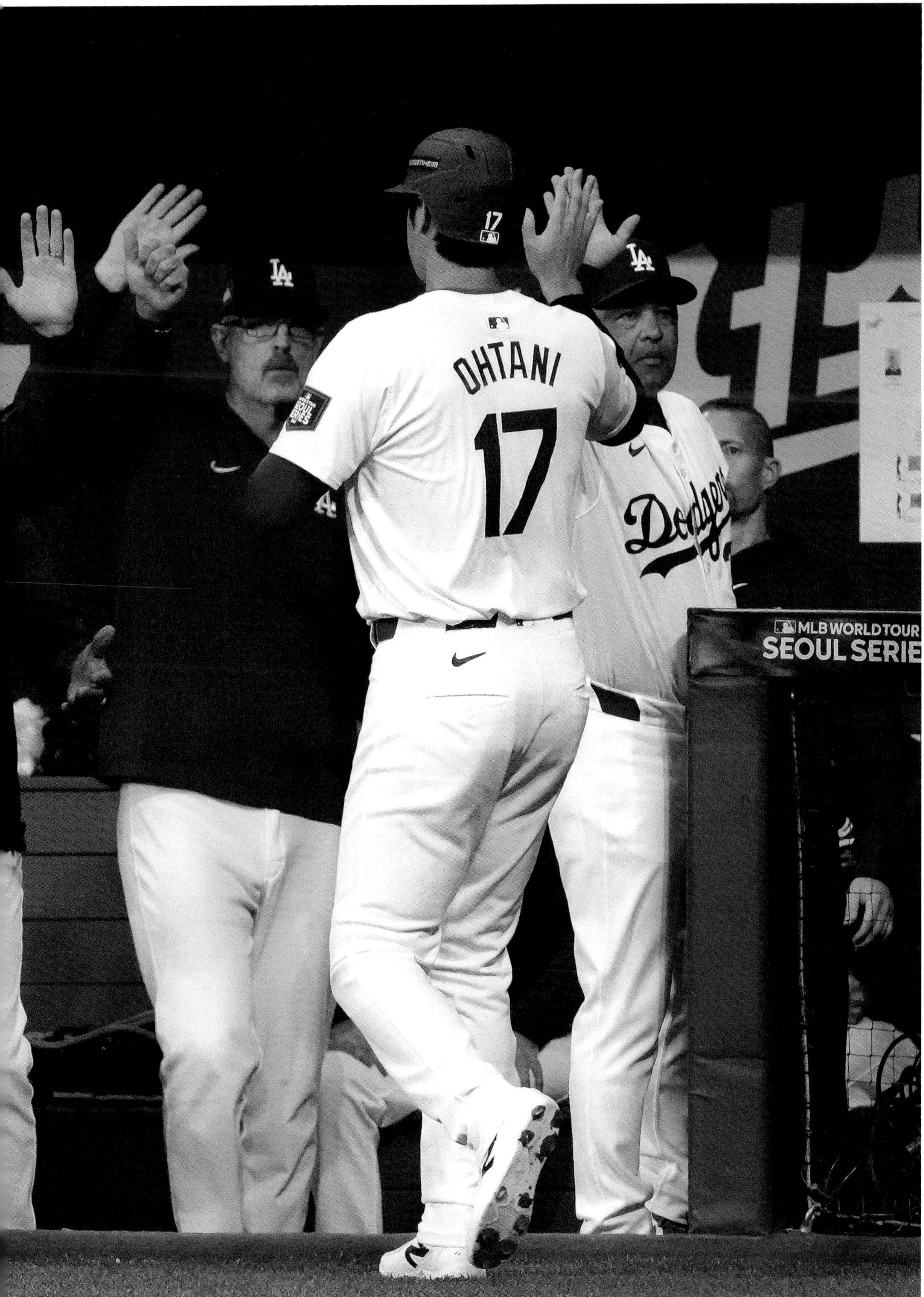
OHTANI
17
Dodgers
MLB WORLD TOUR
SEOUL SERIE

Worth the Wait

Dodgers Sweep Giants as Ohtani Homers for First Time as a Dodger

By Jim Alexander | April 4, 2024

This was what the Dodgers, and their fans, and pretty near all of L.A. and maybe all of baseball – and, definitely, Shohei Ohtani – had been waiting for.

For the first eight games of the season, baseball's unicorn had been strangely muted. In an offense that had been averaging 6.2 runs and hadn't scored less than five runs in a game, the most heralded and expensive acquisition (albeit with deferred money) of the offseason had been, in the words of Manager Dave Roberts, "just a tick off" with the bat.

Two at-bats in Wednesday night's series-sweeping 5-4 victory over the rival San Francisco Giants dramatically, and definitively, changed that narrative.

Ohtani wasn't terrible offensively going into Wednesday night. He just wasn't keeping up with the rest of a high-powered offense, with a .242 average, .630 OPS, two doubles, no home runs – this, from a guy who hit an American League-leading 44 for the Angels in 135 games last year and 171 in his first six big league seasons – and eight strikeouts in 33 at-bats.

When he used his legs to beat out a roller to the right side in the second inning, and then scored from first on Will Smith's double into the left field corner, that was a suggestion. And when he turned on a Taylor Rogers sinker in the seventh – a sinker that didn't sink – and hammered it halfway up the right field pavilion, that was a 430-foot, 105.6 mph declaration to Dodger opponents: *I'm here. And you're now in trouble.*

Imagine a batting order already at near-peak efficiency. Now imagine the best player in the world joining the party. Scary enough for you?

"Honestly, I was very relieved that I was able to get my first home run in a while," Ohtani said afterward via interpreter Will Ireton. "Honestly, my swing hasn't been great."

To be precise, he hadn't gone yard in 214 days, or since a first-inning homer Aug. 23 as an Angel against Cincinnati's Andrew Abbott, in the first game of a doubleheader.

Obviously, a lot has happened since then: The injury that ended his season last Sept. 3, the free agency process that led to his becoming a Dodger, the commotion that surrounded his move up the freeway in the nation's second-largest market (and moved, as well, the attention of Japanese baseball fans and a large slice of that country's media).

And, most recently, there was what a reporter referred to delicately as the "interpreter situation" in a question to Roberts, the revelations that former interpreter Ippei Mizuhara owed $4.5 million in gambling debts to an illegal bookie and drew that money out of Ohtani's bank account,

The storm behind those reports has subsided for now, but it would be easy to imagine that it had an effect on Ohtani, even just enough to throw him off a little bit.

"You just never know about a person until they go through some adversity, whether on the field or in this case off the field," Roberts said. "I've learned that, he doesn't – you know, he's unflappable. He really is. ... It might not be the production that we all expect and we know it's going to happen. But as far as his demeanor, the way he comes in every day, he does a good job sort of

Shohei Ohtani was greeted with a shower of sunflower seeds from teammate Teoscar Hernandez after hitting his highly anticipated first home run as a Los Angeles Dodger. (Los Angeles Daily News: Keith Birmingham)

separating the work from the other stuff."

Even without that storm, the process of getting used to a new organization, a new clubhouse and new teammates and the desire to make a good first impression can affect a player's performance, if ever so slightly, and maybe create some anxiety or angst or frustration. But if it has done so with Ohtani, you'd never see it. Indeed, the talk around the Dodgers is that he has been open and engaging in the clubhouse and has maybe had more and better communication with teammates since the change in interpreters.

And maybe our sky-high expectations don't take into account the idea that players do slump, and do get off to slow starts. At some point, if someone's good enough he'll show it. Maybe that's what we got a glimpse of Wednesday night, and what we're about to see unfold on a six-game trip to Chicago and Minneapolis that begins with a day game Friday in Wrigley Field.

"I'm sure there was some relief there," Roberts said of that mammoth home run, noting that even before that Ohtani seemed "very close" to being back in sync, and "even his misses were just off." The at-bat before the home run, he hit a sharp liner at left fielder Michael Conforto that left the bat at 93.5 mph.

"I think there's something to the human nature part of wanting to get off to a good start with a new team, obviously with the contract and things like that," Roberts said. "But, you know, I think most important is that we're winning baseball games. And I think that's something that helps kind of the transition or the weight that you might feel. And so as long as we keep winning, knowing that he's going to perform at some point in time, (Wednesday night) was a really good step."

Ohtani was far from the only one who came out of the evening with a smile on his face. There was, for example, the fan who caught Ohtani's first Dodgers home run. The MLB authenticator verified the significance of the ball, and the fan made sure it got back to Ohtani.

And what was the price?

"A ball, two caps and a bat," Ohtani said.

A small price, indeed. ∎

Ohtani had struggled to make hard contact in his first games as a Dodger. He finally connected on a sinker from Giants reliever Taylor Rogers to kick off an offensive season for the history books. (Los Angeles Daily News: Keith Birmingham)

37

OUTFIELDER

TEOSCAR HERNANDEZ

Seed-Tossing All-Star Has Been an 'Invaluable' Addition

By Bill Plunkett | July 15, 2024

Shohei Ohtani didn't know what to make of it when his best friend on his new team pelted him with sunflower seeds after his first home run this season.

"It was funny – but he got a little bit scared, I think it was, the first time I threw it at him," Teoscar Hernandez recalled with his ever-present smile spreading a little wider. "But after that, he was ready for it, the seeds."

Ohtani has been pelted the most often, thanks to his National League-leading 29 home runs at the All-Star break. But Hernandez's home run celebration has traveled with him from Toronto to Seattle to L.A. – prompting the creation of "Mr. Seeds" T-shirts with Hernandez's smiling face on them.

"It started when I got traded to Toronto," Mr. Seeds said of his origins story. "I got traded in '17. That's when all the teams started celebrating homers and all that stuff. The Blue Jays didn't have anything. At that time they had a contract with a different brand of sunflower seeds – and we had a bunch. So I started throwing and throwing and throwing.

"So everywhere I go that's a thing. When I got here, I asked the guys, 'Hey, when we hit a homer, is it okay if I do this?' They all said, 'Yeah, for sure, for sure.' So I started doing it."

A new way to celebrate home runs is not all Hernandez has brought to the Dodgers. He heads to the All-Star Game for the second time this year – and the Home Run Derby for the first time – second on the Dodgers (behind his friend, Ohtani) in home runs (19) and RBIs (62). No Dodger has driven in more runs with two outs (25) than Hernandez.

Batting behind some combination of fellow All-Stars Ohtani, Mookie Betts, Freddie Freeman and Will Smith, the RBI opportunities have been plentiful for Hernandez — his 108 at-bats with runners in scoring position are second in the majors.

Given how poorly the bottom half of the Dodgers' lineup has performed and how long Max Muncy has been sidelined with a strained oblique muscle, however, Hernandez's level of competence has been essential to the Dodgers' offense.

"He's been invaluable," Dodgers manager Dave Roberts said. "A guy that can go to left field, right field, doesn't bat an eye where he bats in the order, versus left, versus right, 1s and 2s (top pitchers) – he doesn't duck anyone. he's in there. Day game after night game, he's in there. It doesn't matter."

And the Dodgers are getting all this for the low, low price of $15 million down and 10 easy payments of $850,000 each starting in 2030.

The 31-year-old Hernandez had high hopes when he entered free agency for the first time last winter. He hadn't had his best season with the Seattle Mariners in 2023 – which he blames in part on a slow start following his

After teammate and fellow All-Star Shohei Ohtani elected to sit out the 2024 Home Run Derby, Teoscar Hernandez volunteered to take his place. Hernandez would go on to win the contest at Globe Life Field, the first Dodger to accomplish that feat. (AP Photo)

participation in the World Baseball Classic for the Dominican Republic and his discomfort hitting at T-Mobile Park (where he had a .217 batting average and a .643 OPS). But he had expectations of multi-year offers, maybe as much as a four-year deal. Those offers never materialized. He had a two-year offer from the Boston Red Sox. Instead, he signed with the Dodgers for one year and agreed to defer $8.5 million of the salary – essentially putting pressure on himself to perform well enough to make multi-year offers more likely next winter.

"I said I'm going to bet on myself," he said. "With this team, I'm going to have a good season. I'm going to learn. Now that I know the (free agent) process and I know everything, I'm going to be ready if I have to go through it again."

Hernandez would rather not go through it again. He doesn't hesitate to say he would like to continue tossing sunflower seeds as a Dodger beyond this season.

"I don't want to," he said of returning to free agency. "If I got the chance to stay here for two, three years I would like to stay. I like everything that this team, this organization, they do. For me, I'd feel really good if they come to me and offer me an extension."

It remains to be seen how anxious the Dodgers might be to make that offer. The outfielders around Hernandez are largely young – Andy Pages, James Outman and converted infielder Miguel Vargas. But Hernandez doesn't see them as threats to his longevity with the Dodgers. He has embraced a role as mentor.

"It's not that it's my responsibility. It makes me feel good doing it because I didn't have that when I started," said Hernandez, who came up in the Houston Astros' system. "For me, doing things to help others through what I went through, to me it's a blessing. I'm at a point in my career where doing that makes me feel good about myself and the things that I went through. I thank God that I went through that and now I have the power to show others to not let down, to not feel down, to keep going. Because this is not easy.

"I know those guys are going to be the future for this team and they play my position. A lot of people ask me, 'You don't worry about that?' No, I don't care. I don't think about that. I just want the people around me to be good, my teammates to be great and everybody to be good." ∎

Hernandez agreed to a one-year contract with the Dodgers in January 2024, motivated by the opportunity to improve and compete deep into the postseason. (Los Angeles Daily News: Keith Birmingham)

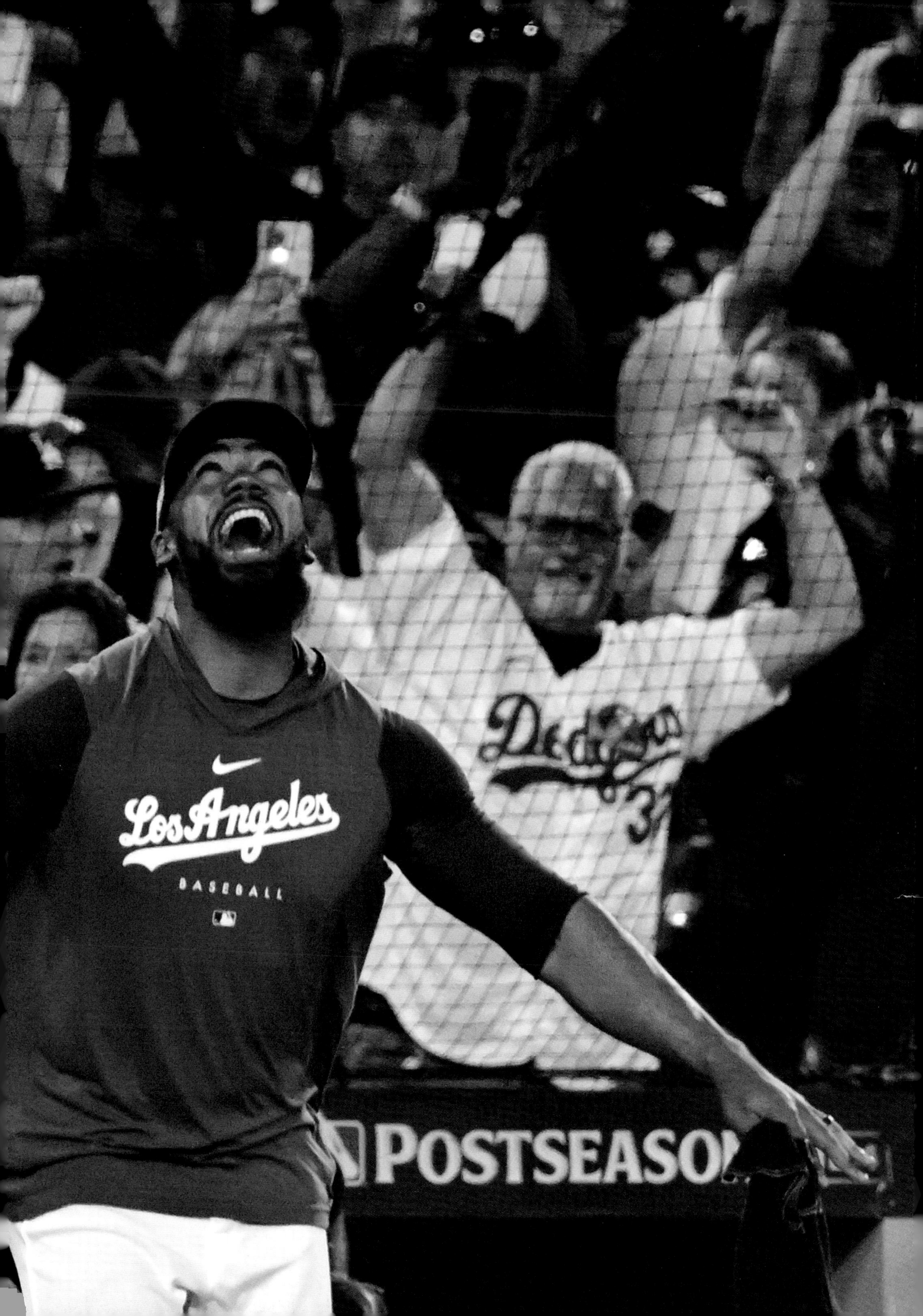

Los Angeles
BASEBALL
POSTSEASON

SECOND BASEMAN

GAVIN LUX

After Missing 2023 Season, Infielder Ditched 'Safe Swings' for 'Doing Damage'

By Bill Plunkett | August 1, 2024

Gavin Lux is learning to trust again.

He was minding his own business one spring afternoon last year, running the bases during a Cactus League game, when his right knee betrayed him. The ACL and LCL had to be repaired by a surgery that kept him out of a batter's box for the next year.

Back on the field this season, Lux's knee was fixed but he still had to recover mentally. His knee might have been healthy but it took longer for his confidence in that knee to return.

The results were what he acknowledges were "safe swings" – the kind that didn't put too much pressure on his knee and put the ball in play but resulted in a lot of ground balls rolled over to the right side or punchless fly outs.

He was putting the ball in play often enough. But it was weak contact.

"I wasn't really locking out on my front leg as hard as I usually do. It was a lot softer," Lux said of his protective mindset – conscious or subconscious. "Then I think early on it was trying not to punch or chase (to strike out). Just trying to put the ball in play. Hit singles and try to get on base where when I feel good it's like, 'Okay, I'm going up there looking to do damage.' Especially those first two strikes then once you get to two strikes you've got to battle your (behind) off.

"I almost feel like I took that two-strike approach from pitch one. I was more being protective instead of saying, '(Expletive) it. We're up there to hurt somebody.' Then once you get to two strikes you shorten up and try to put the ball in play. It was almost like a two-strike mentality from 0-0. You're just trying to survive and you can't do that up here."

In spring training, Dodgers manager Dave Roberts said it would not be fair to judge Lux in his comeback season until he had at least 150 plate appearances under his belt. But Lux was still batting only .207 with a .542 OPS in early July, 264 plate appearances into his season.

That defensive approach was not what made Lux a first-round draft pick or one of the top prospects in baseball. There were times when he wondered if he had forgotten how to hit.

"Some days it felt like that, yeah," he said. "I think in May and even early June it was really searching, searching, searching. There were some days where it was, 'Man, I don't know if I'm going to figure it out.'

"But there's always light at the end of the tunnel. You just try to keep going and chip away. I think I was more patient with myself than I was in past years when I struggled. Just trying to keep a little bit of freshness every day and chip away when you get to the cage."

Gavin Lux celebrates a solo home run against the Los Angeles Angels on June 22. After struggling at the plate early in the season, Lux began to find his stride shortly before the All-Star break and carried that confidence into the second half. (Los Angeles Daily News: Keith Birmingham)

The breakthrough began in the week before the All-Star break.

"I think it was gradual, things coming together. Even when I was struggling we still chipped away, put together some pieces that we felt would work," Lux said. "Then I think in Philly (the final road trip before the All-Star break) it was, 'I'm sick of rolling over. Let's try to do damage.'"

Lux carried that mentally with him when he went home for the All-Star break and spent time with his uncle, Augie Schmidt. The Golden Spikes winner as the top amateur player in 1982 and the second overall pick in that year's draft, Schmidt never made the major leagues, making him very familiar with the ups and downs of a baseball career. Head baseball coach at Carthage College in Wisconsin since 1988, he has been a baseball mentor for Lux.

"I talk to him a ton. But obviously he's not here so it was tough to get a gauge on what I was doing every day, what I was feeling in the batter's box," Lux said. "We'd talk about it. But I think going back home during the All-Star break and getting to sit down and talk about hitting for a couple hours then go out and mess around with some things and just have a lot of free time to try a couple things, see what feels good, what doesn't, where during the season you've got a game to play, you've got a million different things to do it's hard to find that time. So I think the All-Star break helped a lot."

Lux came out of the break and won the National League Player of the Week award. Since that pre-break series in Philadelphia, Lux has hit .385 (20 for 52) with a 1.162 OPS in 18 games. Most significantly, he has nine extra-base hits in that time (five doubles, four home runs) almost matching his total from his first 74 games of the season (12).

At a time when the Dodgers are searching for any offensive contributions they can get from a lineup stripped of Mookie Betts, Freddie Freeman and Max Muncy, Lux has "stepped up," Roberts said. The biggest difference is "confidence" and Lux had to get there on his own.

"I think Brandon McDaniel, the training staff, you can tell him all you want (that his knee is healed), but the player has got to trust that when they're in that moment. And watching him right now, he's playing and moving as well as I've remembered," Roberts said.

"What do they say? It takes a village. So it's a lot of people, but most important it's him to listen and trust it."

Lux acknowledges that it took "a mental shift" to stop thinking about his knee and getting aggressive instead of protective.

"I think I finally have some mental peace that my knee is going to be fine and whatever happens, happens, I can't control it," he said. "If it happens again, I'm going to go down aggressive. That's just kind of the type of approach I've taken with that, too.

"I go back and look at old videos when I feel good and the gather and the load and the swing looks a little more like if you're playing in the backyard as opposed to just being safe. I think just looking at that, that stood out to me."

And why did it take so long?

"There's probably a couple different things," Lux said. "Obviously not playing for a whole year doesn't help. Then you don't get results out of the gate. You kind of start searching for things. I've fallen into this before where you don't get results so you try to look for things that are wrong. It kind of snowballs, snowballs, snowballs. Obviously didn't play for a year then the mental grind of baseball. A lot of it is just trying to find some confidence in the batter's box." ∎

Gavin Lux fields a ninth-inning drive during a win over the Pittsburgh Pirates on August 9.
(Los Angeles Daily News: David Crane)

#MaxStrong

Freddie Freeman Returns to Dodgers After 3-Year-Old Son's Health Scare

By Doug Padilla | August 5, 2024

Throughout an emotional 30-minute press conference on Monday, Dodgers first baseman Freddie Freeman broke down multiple times as he detailed the health ordeal that his 3-year-old son Maximus has endured over the past two weeks.

After missing the Dodgers' entire eight-game road trip that concluded Sunday at Oakland, Freeman is back with the club and was batting in the No. 3 spot of the order Monday against the Philadelphia Phillies.

What Freeman could not guarantee is that his mind would not wander from time to time.

Freeman's son first was diagnosed with transient synovitis following a recent illness. But when Max's health continued to decline, a further examination last week revealed Guillain-Barré syndrome, which caused temporary paralysis and forced the youngster to be intubated in order to breathe.

"It's a good thing I'm here, because it means things are trending better. (For wife) Chelsea and I, it's been a long week," Freeman said before starting to fight back tears. "No one should have to go through this, especially a 3-year-old. I don't know how many times Chelsea and I said we wish we could switch (places with Max)."

Max's symptoms started to become serious during the Dodgers' July 22-25 home series against the San Francisco Giants. The Freemans noticed Max walking with a limp on the morning of Monday (July 22) and by that night, Max couldn't walk. The symptoms, according to an initial visit to a doctor, were consistent with transient synovitis, which can cause a pain in the hip after a viral infection.

The next day, Max couldn't sit up, and by that Wednesday night, he had stopped eating and drinking and was taken to the emergency room. Doctors still suspected transient synovitis and recommended Tylenol.

Freeman played in an afternoon game against the Giants on that Thursday (July 25), and thinking his son was on the road to recovery, he then traveled with the Dodgers to Houston that night. Following a pregame workout on July 26, he scrambled to get back to Southern California after Max's condition "rapidly declined," according to a family Instagram post, and he was sent to the emergency room.

At Children's Hospital of Orange County last week, Max was diagnosed with Guillain-Barré, an autoimmune disorder where the immune system begins to attack the nervous system. In Max's case, the onset of paralysis, starting at the feet and progressing quickly up the body to the shoulders, affected breathing.

More than a week after his health began to deteriorate, Max's condition began to improve with an intravenous immunoglobulin treatment administered over a 24-hour period. While improved, and with much of his mobility returned, Freeman's son now must undergo

Freddie Freeman took a leave of absence when his son Max was hospitalized with symptoms of Guillain-Barré syndrome, an autoimmune disorder which can cause paralysis. (AP Images)

physical therapy as he learns to walk again.

"Thankfully, we were at CHOC hospital in Orange County; absolutely incredible team of doctors," Freeman said. "There's just no words to thank Dr. (Jason) Knight and his staff in the PICU unit. The nurses day and night, absolutely incredible. The respiratory therapists, neurology, every department, I can't. I mean, I'm here nine days after and it feels like a miracle, it really does. So I can't thank them enough."

Freeman said that while he does not have a complete timetable, his son is expected to make a full recovery.

Those who reached out to the Freeman family included Milwaukee Brewers manager Pat Murphy and staff, Arizona Diamondbacks manager Torey Lovullo and the Atlanta Braves organization. And Freeman was especially grateful to the Dodgers organization from President of Baseball Operations Andrew Friedman, Manager Dave Roberts, controlling owner Mark Walter and President/CEO Stan Kasten.

"I just can't thank the baseball community (enough)," Freeman said. "And I'm sure there's people that aren't even in the baseball community that are sending well wishes and prayers our way and support and love. We needed it all. We can't thank everyone enough during this time."

Throughout pregame preparations on Monday, every Dodgers player wore a blue T-shirt with "#MaxStrong" on the front and Freeman's name and No. 5 on the back.

"That was the first time I cried today, when I walked in and saw those (shirts)," Freeman said. "It means a lot."

The toughest part of the ordeal for Freeman was watching his son needing assistance to breathe, reminding him of the agony when he was 10 and his mother passed away from melanoma.

"I know Dodger fans won't like this, but I would gladly strike out with the base loaded in the bottom of the night inning, in Game 7 of the World Series 300 million times in a row, than see that again," said Freeman, an eight-time All-Star who had started every one of the team's first 104 games. "But he's on his way. He's on his way. It's gonna be a long road, but hopefully by next season, spring training, you'll see him on family day doing normal things."

Maximus is one of the Freemans' three sons. Charlie is the oldest, followed by Brandon and Maximus, a name Chelsea came upon.

"That was a strong name," Freeman said. "I didn't know it was going to be proven to be true within four years of his life of how strong this little boy is."

Freeman entered Monday night's game with a .288 batting average, an .888 OPS, 16 home runs, 26 doubles and 67 RBIs this season.

To make room on the active roster for Freeman's return, utility man Cavan Biggio was designated for assignment. Biggio, 29, hit .192 with three homers and 10 RBIs in 30 games for the Dodgers after being acquired on June 12 from Toronto. ■

Teammates, personnel and fans showed their support for Freeman and his family, wearing #MaxStrong shirts and greeting the Dodgers first baseman with a standing ovation upon his return. (AP Images)

DESIGNATED HITTER

SHOHEI OHTANI

Dodgers' International Man of History Reaches 50-50 Milestone

By Bill Plunkett | September 20, 2024

Just a unicorn doing unicorn things.

It wasn't enough for Shohei Ohtani to become baseball's first 50-50 man. He upped the ante to 51-51 and arrived at the unprecedented heights with the biggest game of his career, one of the best offensive games by any hitter in baseball history.

Ohtani had a career-high six hits on Thursday – including two doubles and home runs in each of his final three at-bats – with 10 RBIs and two stolen bases as the Dodgers pounded the Miami Marlins, 20-4. The win clinched a postseason berth for the Dodgers for the 12th consecutive season.

Only the sixth player in baseball history to have 40 home runs and 40 stolen bases in the same season – and the fastest to get there – Ohtani is the first player to then go on to reach 50 in each category.

More importantly to Ohtani, the win will take his name off another list. He has currently played more games (865) without making a postseason appearance than any other active player.

"He's one of one," Dodgers manager Dave Roberts said of Ohtani.

"We all know we witnessed history," Dodgers infielder Miguel Rojas said.

"That has to be the greatest baseball game of all time. It has to be," Dodgers second baseman Gavin Lux said. "There's no way. It's ridiculous. I've never seen anybody do that even in little league, so it's crazy that he's doing that at the highest level."

Ohtani has certainly shown a flair for the dramatic during this historic season. He reached the 40-40 milestone with a walk-off grand slam against the Tampa Bay Rays on Aug. 23. He reached the 50-50 mark – and passed it – with the first three-homer game of his career, the first six-hit game of his career and a Dodgers' franchise record 10 RBIs (also a career high for the two-time MVP).

Ohtani is the first player in MLB history to have a six-hit, three-homer, 10-RBI game – not to mention the two steals.

"Take the season out of it – today was probably the single best offensive game I've ever seen," Dodgers third baseman Max Muncy said. "What did he have – six hits, 10 RBIs, three home runs? And don't forget he had two or three stolen bases today also – yeah, why not?

"That's insane."

It's impossible to "take the season out of it." It has been historic.

With a blast against the Marlins, Shohei Ohtani became the first player in MLB history to reach at least 50 homers and 50 stolen bases in a season. (AP Images)

"Just happy, relieved and very respectful to the peers and everybody that came before that played this sport of baseball," Ohtani said through his interpreter.

"If I'm being honest, it was something I wanted to get over as soon as possible because the balls were being exchanged (for specially marked baseballs) every time I was up to bat, so it was something that I wanted to get over with."

He got it over with at loanDepot Park – the same place where Team Japan won the 2023 World Baseball Classic championship game with Ohtani closing it out.

"I've had perhaps the most memorable moments here in my career," Ohtani joked. "And this stadium has become one of my favorite stadiums."

After the game, the Dodgers (91-62) celebrated clinching a postseason berth with a team champagne toast. Roberts, whose team is four games ahead of the San Diego Padres (87-66) in the NL West and two games ahead of the Milwaukee Brewers (88-65) for a top-two seed and a first-round bye in the NL playoffs, spoke to the team and so did Ohtani.

"He was just really grateful to his teammates for their support," Roberts said. "That's about it. A man of few words."

The two stolen bases came quickly Thursday, one each in the first two innings, giving Ohtani 51 for the season (the 13th season of 50 or more stolen bases in Dodgers history). He doubled in his first at-bat and stole third base, just beating the throw to get No. 50. He scored on a sacrifice fly by Will Smith.

He came up with two on and two out in the second inning and drove in a run with a single – then stole second base for his 51st steal of the season.

The Dodgers scored five times in the third inning against Marlins starter Edward Cabrera who hit a batter and walked three batters in a row, forcing two of the runs home. Ohtani came up with two on and two out again and laced a line drive into the left-center field gap to drive in two runs. He was thrown out trying to stretch it into a triple.

"He almost got the cycle in four at-bats," Rojas said in amazement. "If the cutoff man throws the ball away a little bit, he's got a cycle in four at-bats. And then he got three homers, six hits, it's pretty unbelievable."

The Dodgers have scored four runs or more in an inning in each of the past five games – and they did it three times Thursday.

Ohtani's next at-bat came in the sixth inning with one on and one out. He destroyed an 0-and-1 slider from Marlins reliever George Soriano, hitting it 111.2 mph on a line into the second deck in right field, an estimated 438 feet away.

Outfielder Mookie Betts was asked if he was afraid to say anything to Ohtani about getting to 50 after hitting his 49th home run.

"No," Betts said. "I don't think you can jinx greatness like that."

According to statistician Sarah Langs, that made Ohtani just the second player since 1920 with three extra-base hits, five RBIs and multiple stolen bases in a single game.

And he wasn't done.

Four consecutive Dodgers reached base with one out in the seventh inning. Two scored on a double by Andy Pages. The runners held at second and third when Chris Taylor grounded out, leaving first base open when Ohtani came up.

Trailing 11-3 at the time, Marlins manager Skip Schumaker let reliever Mike Baumann pitch to Ohtani rather than intentionally walking him. On the broadcast, Schumaker could be seen saying to someone in the Marlins' dugout, "(Expletive) that. I've got too much respect for this guy for that (an intentional walk) to happen."

"A lot of us actually looked into the opposing dugout and I think a lot of the coaches were telling Skip, 'Hey, we should walk him here,'" Muncy said. "I have no idea what was actually said over there but that's how it looked. You could kind of tell Skip was, 'I can't do that.' So tip of the cap to Skip right there for letting him hit.

During the 2024 season Shohei Ohtani showed off his speed like never before, blowing away his previous season high of stolen bases of 26 with 59 swiped bags. (Los Angeles Daily News: Keith Birmingham)

"We all saw it coming, I think. He was just in that zone."

Ohtani swung at the first two pitches, fouling them off then took a ball high for a 1-and-2 count. Baumann offered up a knuckle curve and Ohtani took it the opposite way, sending it over the wall in left field for his historic 50th home run.

The sparse crowd – announced as 15,548 and featuring a high percentage of Dodger fans – gave Ohtani a standing ovation. He stepped out of the dugout and waved to the crowd in acknowledgement.

"I think that's a bad move – baseball-wise, karma-wise, baseball gods-wise. You go after him and see if you can get him out," Schumaker said afterward when asked about walking Ohtani. "I think out of respect for the game we were going to go after him. He hit the home run. That's just part of the deal. He's hit 50 of them.

"It was a good day for baseball. But a bad day for the Marlins."

Down 14-3 when the ninth inning started, the Marlins sent out infielder Vidal Brujan to pitch. He hit the first batter he faced. Two batters later, he gave up a two-out single to Taylor, turning the Dodgers' lineup over and bringing Ohtani to the plate again.

He watched two of Brujan's fastballs float past then turned on a 68.3 mph offering, sending it 440 feet into the upper deck in right field for his 51st home run of the season.

"I don't even know if it was like a relief thing," Betts said of Ohtani's mood after reaching 50-50. "I think he was just feeling good, feeling sexy and just knew, like, 'I'm about to do this today.' I mean, he could've had four homers today. I'm at a loss for words." ∎

Shohei Ohtani tips his helmet to the home crowd at Dodger Stadium as they cheer a day after he made history with the first 50-50 season in MLB history. (Los Angeles Daily News: Keith Birmingham)

Champagne and Crutches

Freeman Injures Ankle as Dodgers Clinch National League West Crown

By Jim Alexander | September 27, 2024

Maybe it was fitting, in a grisly sort of way. All season the Dodgers have shrugged off injuries – including seven projected starting pitchers to the injured list – and they've faced a strong September challenge for only the third time in the 12 straight seasons they've reached the playoffs.

And wouldn't you know it? The night they beat the San Diego Padres to clinch the National League West, another key player goes down. When Freddie Freeman severely rolled his ankle trying to evade a tag at first base in the seventh inning on Thursday night, after the Dodgers had wiped out a 2-0 deficit with a five-run rally en route to a 7-2 victory, it brought back the grisly memories of Max Muncy hurting his arm in a collision at first on the final day of the 2021 season, rendering him unavailable for the playoffs.

But it could have been much worse. X-rays taken Thursday night were negative. Freeman, who was on crutches and wearing a walking boot during the Dodgers' locker room celebration, figures to sit out the final regular-season series in Colorado this weekend, and the division championship and first-round bye give him eight days to heal before the Division Series begins here next Saturday.

The injury list has been so crowded this season it might as well have a turnstile, so what else is new? Relievers Brusdar Graterol (shoulder inflammation) and Brent Honeywell (cracked fingernail) went on the injured list before Thursday night's game, though the latter might

have been a procedural move to get Anthony Banda back on the active roster.

But consider that said injured list also includes Tyler Glasnow, Clayton Kershaw, Gavin Stone, Dustin May, River Ryan, Emmet Sheehan and Tony Gonsolin. Of those, Gonsolin – a year removed from Tommy John surgery – might be the most likely to actually see the mound in the postseason.

So when the Dodgers, with their massive payroll commitments and with a major league-best 95 victories going into the final weekend, draw the old adversity card … well, it's not totally bogus, even if few on the outside buy it.

"What an accomplishment," Dodgers president of baseball operations Andrew Friedman said Thursday night, off to the side of the champagne-soaked clubhouse celebration, his face dusted with baby powder after Kiké Hernandez ambushed him.

"The fight from this group, just the adversity that we faced throughout the year, (and) to take two of three (from the Padres) the hard way, losing the first game and watching Walker (Buehler) tonight, reminiscent of a lot of big games we've seen him pitch in this stadium. Our bullpen was phenomenal. I can't say enough about this group one through 26."

Buehler was the ace-in-waiting the last time the Dodgers clinched a division title at home with fans in the stands, when he strode to the mound for Game 163 against Colorado in 2018 and acted like he owned it. A

Relief pitcher Michael Kopech celebrates after getting the final out to clinch the National League West Division title. (Los Angeles Daily News: Keith Birmingham)

second Tommy John surgery set him back, and he started this season late and went on the IL again in June with hip inflammation. Even after returning in August, he was inconsistent enough to cast doubt on his ability to contribute in the postseason.

Thursday night's clincher might have restored some of others' confidence in him: Five innings, five hits, one run and that old "I run this" attitude.

"I mean, with Walker the arrow has been pointing up all year," Friedman said. "It was a little rocky there in the beginning, but the stuff was there. It was about the execution. What we knew all along was that … he doesn't shy away from the moment. He's not scared of anything and he's going to go out and compete."

Buehler's confidence in big moments has been evident all along. So has that of Shohei Ohtani, but only in small doses in the World Baseball Classic. Now he will get the October spotlight, and if the Dodgers are to make this a deep run and a potentially memorable postseason, it will be up to a guy who will be getting his first taste of October baseball.

He might be made for it. When he came up in the seventh Thursday night with one out and the go-ahead run on second, didn't you just have a feeling that he was going to get that run in?

Dave Roberts did.

"No doubt in my mind," the manager said. "I just think he's determined. He's going to will himself to help us win baseball games."

He did, of course, rolling a ground ball through the right side for a single, moving up on Fernando Tatis Jr.'s throwing error in an attempt to get lead runner Andy Pages at third, and scoring on Mookie Betts' two-run single to make it 5-2.

This is something we've learned since Shohei joined the Dodgers, where the big games and big moments are far more plentiful than they were in Anaheim: He maintains an even greater focus in those moments when the place is going crazy.

"I felt like the environment really elevated my performance, and it allowed me to be focused through my whole at-bat," Ohtani said through interpreter Will Ireton. "I felt like I was really so focused that I didn't have the opportunity to feel nervous."

Do you get the impression, then, that not only is Ohtani perfect for the big stage, but that those six seasons with the Angels were in some ways a waste of his talents?

Or that, in his first playoffs in the big leagues, he'll carry this club with him as necessary?

"I think that there are some people that when the moment gets big, they run from it," Roberts said. "Other guys embrace it. And Shohei has embraced these moments better than any player I've ever been around."

He might need some work at this champagne celebration frenzy, but that would be considered a first-world problem.

Otherwise, there will be a lot to embrace going forward. Going into the final weekend in Colorado the Dodgers are a game ahead of Philadelphia and two ahead of the AL East champion New York Yankees in the race for the game's best record, even with an ever-shifting starting rotation that has placed more of a burden on their bullpen than any other team in the game. The bye during the wild-card round, which seemed to be an impediment the last two seasons, will at least give them a chance to figure out what their playoff rotation might look like.

"We like high expectations," Friedman said. "We relish 'em. It beats the (expletive) out of the alternative, and people just not caring. So people care. They're passionate about the Dodgers. They have high expectations. So do we. We think that's a great thing. And for us, this is step one."

And there will be only one satisfactory outcome, and no excuses. Everyone in the Dodger organization understands that. ∎

Catcher Will Smith is showered in sunflower seeds after tying the game with a two-run home run in the seventh inning. (Los Angeles Daily News: Keith Birmingham)

PITCHER

JACK FLAHERTY

Dodgers' Hometown Hero Dreams of a Hollywood Ending

By Mirjam Swanson | October 5, 2024

Jack Flaherty's story has so many elements of a classic coming-of-age sports movie that you almost feel like you should be able to predict the ending.

The best player on the "Sandlot" growing up to play for the Dodgers? It being set in the Valley, a la "Karate Kid" and "Bad News Bears"? The backdrop being a famously competitive Little League that produced TV stars like Tom Selleck and All-Stars like Jack McDowell, that was dominated for a spell by a pitcher who damn right threw like a girl, the real-life Amanda Whurlitzer – known to Flaherty and his generation as Marti Sementelli.

Those Sherman Oaks Little Leaguers remember her, and she remembers them too – Flaherty especially: "One of those kids that was like, 'You gotta watch out for him, 'cause he's gonna be something.'"

I imagine everyone who played with or against that famously intense little Flaherty fellow remembers, and that they've all been tuned in since July, when he was traded from Detroit to L.A., a Boy in Blue at 28.

That they'll be on the edge of their seats watching him take the mound in Game 2 of the National League Division Series at Dodger Stadium, the site of Harvard-Westlake High School's CIF Southern Section Division I championship in 2017, when Flaherty singled in the game's only run and pitched an eight-strikeout shutout.

Not sure how far we can push this dream sequence before producers reject the script as being too far-fetched, but it feels like Flaherty is eager to find out.

Because when Mookie Betts had Flaherty on his podcast and mentioned "how tough it's going to be" to have to perform in the postseason in front of the hometown fans, the pitcher shook him off: "Yeah, it's fun."

"That's what you qualify as fun?" Betts asked. (The two-time World Series winner and 2018 American League MVP who's slumped in his past couple postseasons used a different word: "Stress.")

"Yeah, 100%, that's what it is… it's fun, man," said Flaherty, who is 1-3 with an 3.60 ERA in five postseason appearances with the St. Louis Cardinals and Baltimore Orioles. "It's going to be high-intensity, pressure-filled, like, a lot of fun."

Cinema, you might say.

Since joining the Dodgers, the right-hander has a 3.58 ERA in 55⅓ innings over 10 starts, wielding his slider and perhaps his most noteworthy ability – availability.

"I think everyone deep down wants to play for their hometown team," Flaherty told reporters after being traded. "Getting the opportunity to is just special."

It's been special for his oldest fans too, people like Jason Drantch, who played with Flaherty on a different Dodgers team – the one that won the District 40 Little League Tournament of Champions title in 2005.

Jack Flaherty (center), who grew up in Southern California, celebrates with teammates Mookie Betts (left) and Miguel Rojas after the Dodgers' win over the New York Mets to clinch the National League Pennant. (Los Angeles Daily News: Keith Birmingham)

Flaherty was the youngest – 8 or 9 – and best and most intense player on that team, recalled Drantch, a former first baseman who was, at 11, the oldest.

"It was pretty clear at that young age that he had a future in the game," said Drantch, who gives the Dodgers two thumbs-up for changing their minds and deciding to give Flaherty the Game 2 start, because that's the game for which Drantch has tickets.

"When he was on the mound, I just remember the fear the other kids seemed to have. That intensity, he brought that to the mound and you did not want to face him; you did not want to step into the box against him. I'm glad I didn't have to, because it didn't look fun.

"That team we were on, we were very successful," added Drantch, now a sports producer at KTLA. "And that was because of him. He led the way in that regard and it was a great honor to be a part of it."

Sementelli was a couple years older than Flaherty and didn't face him until high school, as she continued her historic baseball career into college and then with Team USA.

She also remembers Flaherty's heart-on-his-sleeve passion, and his prowess at shortstop and as a hitter before he narrowed his focus to pitching in high school – a decision that worked out well, as she watched first-hand this season.

When Flaherty threw 6⅔ innings of no-hit ball May 30 at Fenway Park, Sementelli was there, in the press box, working as one of Major League Baseball's data operations staffers.

"I'm inputting all the live-game updates into the MLB website, tracking every single pitch … and thinking, 'How ironic, that we both came from Sherman Oaks, playing really competitive Little League baseball,'" she said. "'And how cool would it be if I worked Jack Flaherty's no-hitter?'"

She could have imagined he'd have nights like that, she said. But watching him now, it's his staying power that really impresses her: "Not just to make the majors, but to be very successful? Making The Show and being someone that people want on your team, that's a big-time pitcher? He's become that guy in the majors. That's super cool."

"And it isn't easy, no matter how good you are," said Harvard-Westlake athletic director Matt LaCour, who in 2021 became only high school coach to have three former teammates make opening-day starts in the same season, when Flaherty (St. Louis Cardinals), Lucas Giolito (Chicago White Sox) and Max Fried (Atlanta Braves) did it.

The 34th overall pick out of high school in 2014, Flaherty made his big-league debut in 2017 and in 2019 logged a 2.75 ERA in 196⅓ innings and finished fourth in NL Cy Young award voting.

He wasn't as sharp in the short 2020 season and then was hindered by shoulder issues. He still didn't have his best stuff in 2023, when the Cardinals traded him to the Baltimore Orioles, who moved him to the bullpen.

"How you adapt and how you persevere is how you're ultimately going to be successful," LaCour said. "And the way Jack has done, it's a great reminder to guys that are younger … you're going to hit a spot where you're not the best, or people have caught you. It's what you do from there to separate yourself again that's really important."

After signing a one-year, $14 million contract as a free agent last offseason, Flaherty became an All-Star candidate and dependable No. 2 starter for the Tigers, with an 11-8 record and ERA (2.95) that was in the top 10 among AL pitchers.

And then, at the trade deadline, Detroit swapped him for a pair of Dodgers' minor-league prospects.

Now the stage is set, perhaps, for a real-life Hollywood ending. Get your popcorn ready.

"I've had some conversations over the last couple days with some family and some people close to me, just kind of putting it all into perspective and how kind of surreal and just crazy of an opportunity it is – being from here, growing up here, coming to games here," Flaherty said Saturday, before Game 1. "It's just a lot of fun, at the end of the day.

"I was looking back, like little young me, if I was to tell myself this: What would like 8-year-old me say? It would be pretty cool. So I'm just trying to enjoy it." ∎

Jack Flaherty pitches against the Baltimore Orioles on August 27. The Dodgers acquired the Harvard-Westlake graduate from the Detroit Tigers at the 2024 trade deadline. (AP Images)

'On a Collision Course'

Dodgers Face Rival Padres in Playoffs Once Again

By Bill Plunkett | October 6, 2024

Seoul-mates in March, the Dodgers and San Diego Padres are together again in October.

"It's crazy – beginning of the season, we faced them. End of the season, we faced them (in a key September series). Playoffs, we face them again," Dodgers relief pitcher Alex Vesia said. "They have a good ballclub. I think it's going to be a great series. I think it's going to be some of the best baseball you're going to see in the playoffs."

After their workout, including a sim game, on Wednesday, the Dodgers stayed together, gathering in the Stadium Club to watch the Padres beat the Atlanta Braves to advance to the best-of-five National League Division Series. They had a rooting interest – sort of.

"I think everyone was rooting for a third game," Dodgers president of baseball operations Andrew Friedman said with a smile. "As far as who it was, I think more agnostic about that than it going three (games) and chaos and using the 'pen and all kinds of things that can come from being a wild card, and not getting the bye. So much more focused toward that."

Friedman did acknowledge that the Dodgers and Padres seemed to have been "on a collision course" all year.

"Yeah, the last couple years with them being really good and us being really good, we're always going to have to play each other in the playoffs the way our teams are set up," Dodgers second baseman Gavin Lux said. "I think we kind of expected to play San Diego anyways, especially with (Braves ace Chris) Sale going down.

"I don't think any of us wanted anybody to win. It didn't really matter. You have to beat the best teams either way. So embrace the competition."

This is the third time in five years that the Dodgers and Padres have met in the postseason. The Dodgers swept the Padres in three games in an NLDS in the 2020 bubble in Arlington, Texas, then the Padres eliminated the 111-win Dodgers in four games in 2022.

This year, they split the two games in South Korea but the Padres dominated the season series, winning six of the next eight meetings. But the Dodgers took two of three at Dodger Stadium in the final week of the season to clinch their 11th division title in the past 12 years.

That three-game series in September with the division on the line gives the Dodgers something positive to take into this NLDS matchup.

"I think that's important," Lux said. "They kind of kicked our ass all year. So to have them come here in some meaningful games where it felt like a playoff game where the last few years it didn't really matter, I think that only helps. You build the intensity up and it doesn't feel like you're just jumping into a playoff atmosphere. The last few weeks have kind of been that with all these games being meaningful so I think that helps."

Infielder Miguel Rojas agreed, calling it "preparation" for both teams.

"Especially for us," he said. "Also facing their staff is going to be beneficial for us because we're going to be facing them again at this time of the year. Pitchers don't look the same when they're starting the year and when they're pitching meaningful games in September."

In the celebration after their Wild Card Series victory, Padres third baseman Manny Machado was asked about the matchup with the Dodgers in the NLDS and said, "This is what everyone wanted."

He would get no argument from the Dodgers.

"I would agree. I don't think that's a false statement," Vesia said. "If you want to be the best, you have to play good baseball. It's going to be fun." ∎

Fernando Tatis Jr. and the Padres were a familiar division foe for the Dodgers. (Los Angeles Daily News: Keith Birmingham)

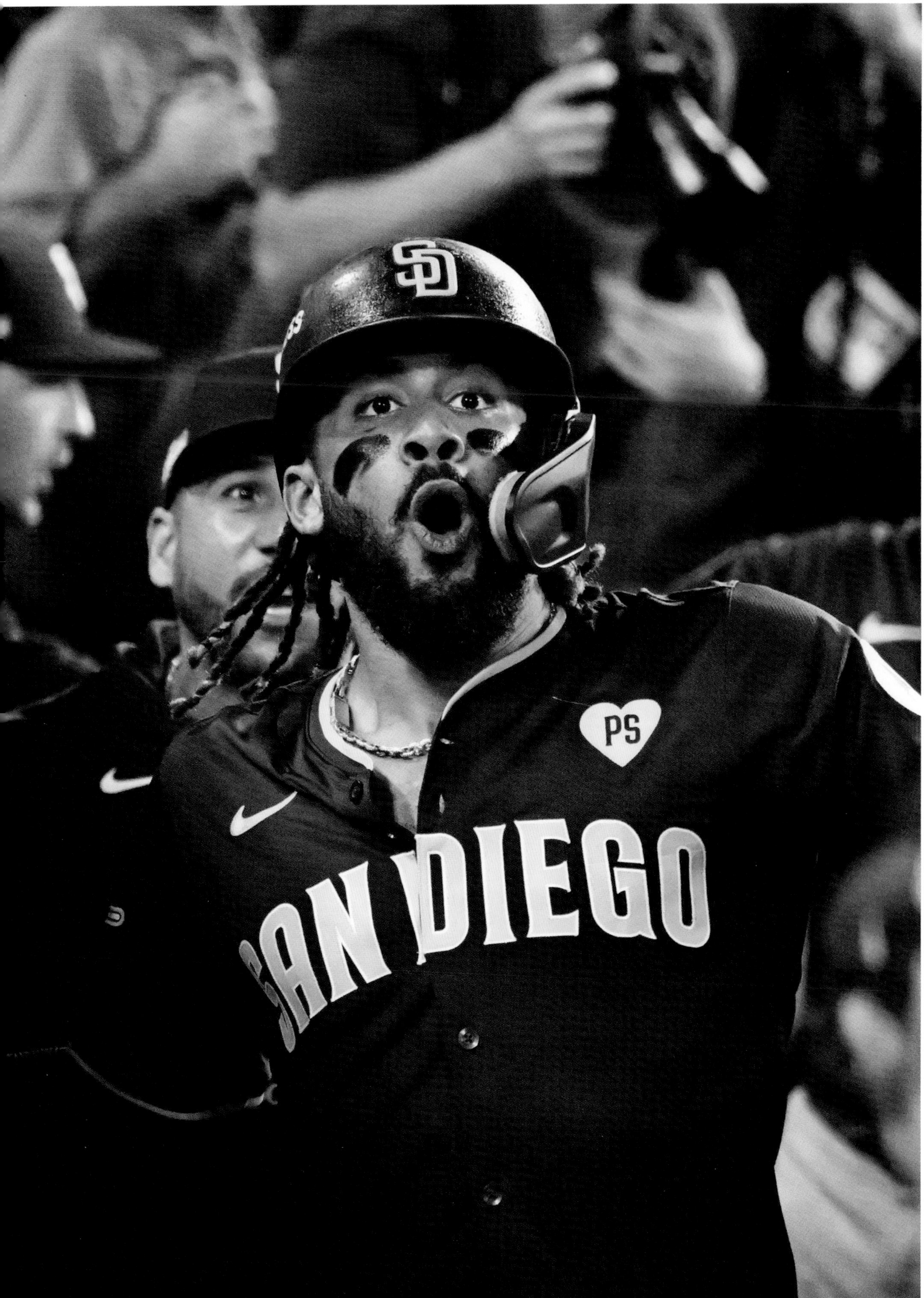
SD
PS
SAN DIEGO

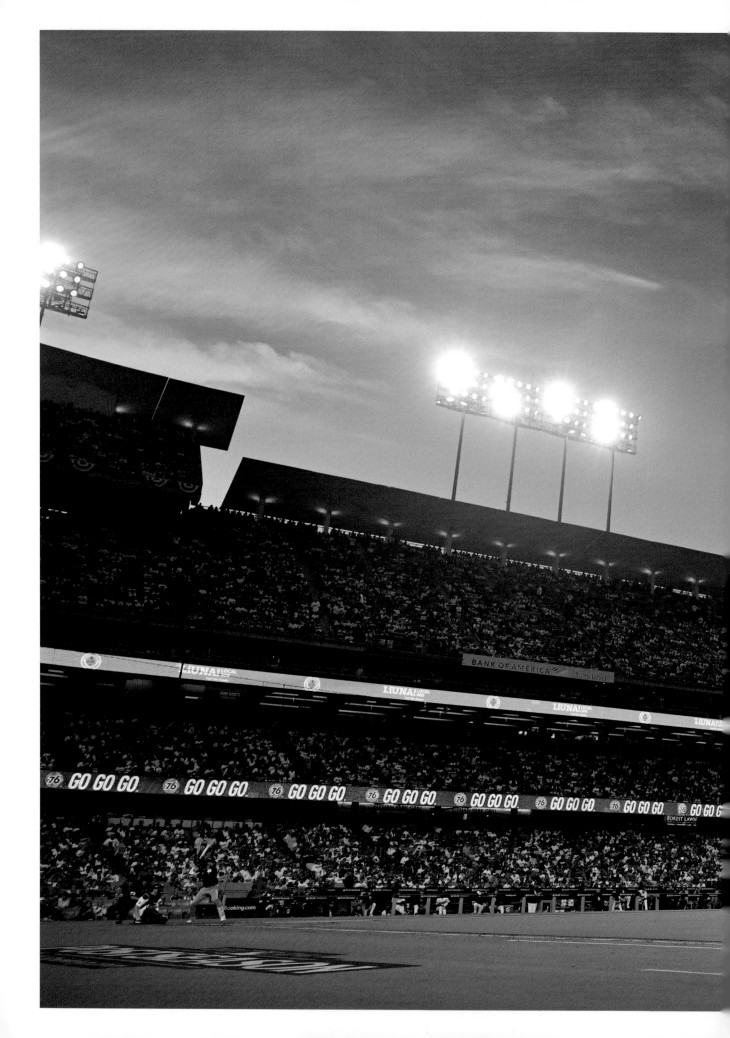

NLDS

NATIONAL LEAGUE DIVISION SERIES GAME 1
October 5, 2024 | Los Angeles, California
DODGERS 7, PADRES 5

Déjà Blue

Dodgers Bullpen Saves the Day Against Familiar Foes

By Bill Plunkett

October history threatened to repeat itself. But the Dodgers had an answer.

Nope.

The San Diego Padres scored five times in three innings against Dodgers starter Yoshinobu Yamamoto. But the Dodgers responded in ways they hadn't when put in the same predicament in last year's postseason. The offense punched back, the bullpen covered for Yamamoto and the Dodgers won Game 1 of their National League Division Series, 7-5, over the Padres Saturday night.

After Yamamoto's three-inning callback to his major-league debut in Korea against the Padres, five Dodgers relievers held the Padres scoreless on two hits over the final six innings. The Dodgers have fallen behind by three runs or more after the first inning of a postseason game 15 times in their history – this was the first time they came back to win.

"I'll ask you about it. What have we done the last month and a half?" Alex Vesia said of the Dodgers' bullpen's performance. "We've definitely been prepared for it. We're pretty darn good. Just take it one inning at a time. That's all you can do."

The win in Game 1 ended a six-game postseason losing streak for the Dodgers, stretching back to a Game 1 victory over the Padres in their 2022 NLDS.

"We need to fight. And that's what we did tonight," Dodgers manager Dave Roberts said. "We didn't get an ideal start. But guys in the 'pen picked us up and the offense was relentless with their at-bats."

The common theme in the back half of that six-game October losing streak was poor starting pitching. Yamamoto kept it going. The first two batters he faced reached base. A wild pitch and a passed ball set up a run-scoring ground out. Then Manny Machado sent a splitter from Yamamoto into the left-field pavilion for a two-run home run.

It brought back memories of Yamamoto's start against the Padres in the Seoul Series when he lasted just one inning and gave up five runs.

There was a common thread there as well – Roberts said Yamamoto might have been tipping his pitches.

"There's some things that I think we're going to dig into because I think at second base they had some things with his glove and giving away some pitches," Roberts said, echoing an issue that came up this spring. "We're going to clean that up. That's part of baseball. So it's on us to kind of clean that up and not give away what pitch he's going to throw."

If there was a feeling of déjà vu from last year's NLDS, Shohei Ohtani cleared the air – and the fence – with a three-run home run to tie the game in his second postseason at-bat.

"I mean, you could almost feel it in the stadium," Dodgers third baseman Max Muncy said. "Then thankfully we have a guy whose name is Shohei Ohtani and he injected an absolute lightning bolt into the

Manager Dave Roberts reacts after a big out in the close Game 1 win over the Padres.
(Los Angeles Daily News: Keith Birmingham)

stadium. From then on it was, 'Alright, we've got this. This is not the same as years past. We're good.'"

It was an all-around new experience for Ohtani who went 2 for 5 in his first MLB postseason game.

"I could really feel the intensity of the stadium before the game began, and I thoroughly enjoyed it," Ohtani said through his interpreter.

The Padres got to Yamamoto again in the third inning. A leadoff double by Fernando Tatis Jr. and a two-out walk of Jackson Merrill – when a 1-and-2 pitch call went against Yamamoto – set up a two-out, two-run double by Xander Bogaerts.

Over their past four postseason games, Dodgers starting pitchers have recorded a combined total of 23 outs while allowing 18 runs – 12 of those runs in the first inning of the games.

During the between-innings interview on the FOX broadcast, Roberts said that would be "the end of the line" for Yamamoto in Game 1.

It wasn't the end of the line for the Dodgers.

With one out in the bottom of the fourth inning, Tommy Edman beat out a bunt single. Miguel Rojas singled to bring Ohtani up with two on again. This time, Ohtani dropped a broken-bat single into center field to load the bases for Mookie Betts.

A wild pitch brought in Edman and moved the runners up. With the count 2-and-2, the Padres sent Betts to first base with an intentional walk. Freddie Freeman (2 for 5 playing on his injured ankle) bounced into a forceout but Teoscar Hernandez dropped a soft line drive just in front of Merrill in center field.

Two runs scored on the two-out hit – a rarity during their postseason losing streak – and the Dodgers had their first lead in a postseason game since the seventh inning of Game 4 in 2022 against the Padres. They added to it with an unearned run in the fifth inning, again building it from the bottom of their lineup.

The bottom four hitters in the Dodgers' lineup – Will Smith, Gavin Lux, Edman and Rojas – were on base eight times on five hits, two walks and an error (turning the lineup over and forcing the Padres to pitch to Ohtani) and scored four of the Dodgers' runs.

"We knew we're gonna score runs and win a ballgame," Smith said. "They jumped on us, punched us in the mouth. We knew we weren't out of it. Just gotta keep fighting."

The Padres' best record in baseball after the All-Star break featured frequent comebacks and late rallies – Merrill alone had six go-ahead or game-tying home runs in the eighth inning or later. But the Dodgers passed their lead from Ryan Brasier to Alex Vesia and Evan Phillips, retiring 11 consecutive hitters at one point.

But Michael Kopech couldn't find the strike zone. He walked two of the three batters he faced. Roberts went to Blake Treinen who got Bogaerts to pop out before he walked Jake Cronenworth to load the bases – then struck out Solano to strand them all.

The Padres put the tying runs on base with two outs in the ninth, bringing up Machado who homered twice off Treinen during the regular season. He struck out to end the game.

The five-out save was Treinen's longest since a two-inning effort in Game 5 of the 2021 NL Championship Series – before his November 2022 shoulder surgery.

"Once the phone rings (in the bullpen), we just lock it in and focus on what we need to do," Treinen said of the six-inning relief relay. "There's no egos, there's no, 'Why am I here? Why am I not there?' When our name is called, we get our lanes, we go out and execute. We're a tight-knit group. We're very fortunate to have a group of guys pulling on the same rope.

"From a fan's standpoint, I feel like that's gotta be a really fun game to watch. And from a Dodgers standpoint, I'm very grateful we ended up on top." ∎

Shohei Ohtani hit a huge, game-tying three-run home run in the second inning to get the Dodgers on the board. (Los Angeles Daily News: Keith Birmingham)

NATIONAL LEAGUE DIVISION SERIES GAME 2

October 6, 2024 | Los Angeles, California

PADRES 10, DODGERS 2

Fanning the Flames

Intensity Increases as Padres Even NLDS with Decisive 10-2 Win

By Bill Plunkett

Once upon a time, the Dodgers did not consider the San Diego Padres their rivals.

Those days are gone.

In a game featuring taunting and trolling by Padres outfielders Jurickson Profar and Fernando Tatis Jr. and unruly behavior by the Dodgers' fans surrounding them in the pavilion seats, the Padres upped the intensity of this National League Division Series, hit a postseason record-tying six home runs and evened the series with a resounding 10-2 victory over the Dodgers in Game 2.

The Padres are the first team to hit six home runs in a postseason game as the road team.

The best-of-five series will take a breath before resuming at Petco Park on Tuesday night – where decorum will likely be breached once again.

"Look, the first thing is it's unacceptable to be throwing stuff on the field. That's the first thing. That's really all there is to say about it," Dodgers infielder Max Muncy said. "There was other stuff involved but you just can't throw stuff on the field like that. It's frustrating. We understand fans are frustrated with us and this game. But you just can't be throwing stuff on the field."

The "other stuff" that Muncy alluded to was Dodgers starter Jack Flaherty hitting Tatis with a pitch in the sixth inning, chirping between Profar and Dodgers catcher Will Smith (who called Profar "irrelevant" earlier this season) and Padres third baseman Manny Machado and the Dodgers' dugout.

"They didn't like the pitch to Tatis," Flaherty said. "Look, I missed in the first inning and I threw the ball over the middle (on Tatis' first homer). I wasn't going to miss over the plate again. I have no reason to hit a guy

there to start off the sixth. … I'm going in for effect and he didn't get out of the way and it hit him.

"I was fired up after getting Manny out (in the first inning). It's a big spot in the playoffs. That's what happens. I was fired up. Oh well. And then, he did some (stuff) between innings where he tries to throw the ball in our dugout. Everybody catches the tail end of it, of me and him going at it, but I was sitting there for my team. I wasn't going to go at him. He was throwing at our dugout. … I understand it's the postseason, everybody's fired up."

The intensity bubbled over as the Dodgers were set to bat in the bottom of the seventh inning. A ball was thrown from the left field pavilion at Profar – who had been taunting fans since stealing a home run from Mookie Betts during the first inning. He reacted angrily and the umpiring crew gathered in shallow left field where Padres manager Mike Shildt gestured at the fans.

"A hostile environment," Shildt said. "What I got out of it was a bunch of dudes that showed up in front of a big, hostile crowd with stuff being thrown at them and said, 'We're going to talk with our play. We're not going to back down. We're going to elevate our game. We're going to be together and we're going to take care of business.'"

When the Padres tried to return to their positions, debris was tossed onto the field from the right field pavilion with Tatis making gestures at the fans that looked like he was telling them to wipe away their tears.

"It's a show. It's MLB: The Show," Tatis said on the field immediately after the game. "We were giving them a show."

In all, the start of the inning was delayed by about 12 minutes. The Padres clearly relished their heel turn – they put the game away with back-to-back home runs in the eighth inning and scored three more in the ninth (featuring Tatis' second home run of the game).

"Dodger fans, they were just not happy," Tatis said. "They're losing the game, obviously, and just a lot of back and forth. What can I say? I wish they could control it a little bit more their emotions. But at the end of the day I see this as part of a game."

No one was more in control than Padres starting pitcher Yu Darvish, who trapped Dodgers hitters in the spin zone all night.

Darvish dipped into seven different categories on the Statcast pitch chart while holding the Dodgers' offense to just three hits and two walks over seven innings.

Darvish's kitchen sink included 17 sweepers, 16 sliders, 15 curveballs, 12 splitters, six sinkers, five cutters and only 11 four-seam fastballs. He held Dodgers star Shohei Ohtani – who called Darvish his "childhood hero" – hitless in three at-bats.

"We were (expletive)," Muncy said of the Dodgers' lack of offense against Darvish.

"Flush it. Move on. Like I said, we were (expletive) tonight. That's not us as a group. We've been good all year."

Ohtani and Darvish are friends off the field. But Darvish's best friends in Game 2 were his outfielders.

In the first inning, Betts drilled a first-pitch sweeper from Darvish down the line in left field and went into his home run trot. The stadium sound system kicked in the home run fanfare.

But Profar reached into the stands, took the ball away from the fans there and a home run away from Betts. Profar taunted the fans as he strutted away with the ball in his glove – a sign of the trolling yet to come.

Betts was hitless in the game and is now 0 for his past 22 in the postseason.

"They're all outs. So they're all terrible," Betts said when asked about the quality of his at-bats. "I don't know

really what to say about it. I'm giving my best, doing my best. Obviously it's not good enough right now.

"It's really frustrating. But nothing I can really do right now but keep going and hope it turns."

In the fourth inning, Freddie Freeman got one of Darvish's four-seamers and lined it hard into right field over the head of Tatis – who reached up on the run and grabbed it, robbing Freeman of a leadoff extra-base hit. Like Profar, Tatis taunted the fans, dancing to the boos that rained down on him from the right field pavilion.

Just an inning later, Freeman left the game with renewed discomfort in his injured right ankle. Dodgers manager Dave Roberts said Freeman would be re-evaluated before Game 3.

"He was down, really down and just couldn't keep going," Roberts said. "We had no other choice. He's doing everything he can. I don't know what his status will be like for Game 3. But for tonight we had no other option."

Center fielder Jackson Merrill joined the outfield highlight reel in the sixth inning when he went back to the wall to haul in Kiké Hernandez's long fly ball.

The Dodgers had Darvish's own back to the wall in the second inning but let him off the hook. They loaded the bases with no outs. Gavin Lux drove in one run with a sacrifice fly but Tommy Edman lined a ball directly at first baseman Luis Arraez, who then doubled Smith off first to end the inning.

While Darvish was outstanding for the Padres, Flaherty gave the Dodgers their best postseason start in years – a seriously low bar.

Flaherty gave up a solo home run to Tatis in the first inning and a two-run home run to David Peralta in the second. While playing with an elbow injury that he wasn't completely honest with the Dodgers about last season, Peralta didn't hit a home run after July 8.

Flaherty did pitch into the sixth inning – the longest postseason start by a Dodgers pitcher since Max Scherzer went seven innings in Game 3 of the 2021 NLDS against the San Francisco Giants. ∎

NATIONAL LEAGUE DIVISION SERIES GAME 3

October 8, 2024 | San Diego, California

PADRES 6, DODGERS 5

Razor's Edge

Dodgers on Brink of Elimination After Padres Take Game 3 of NLDS

By Bill Plunkett

It's October, time for chills and frights.

And the Dodgers are experiencing déjà boo.

A third consecutive first-round exit could be one day away after the San Diego Padres scored six times in the second inning against Walker Buehler – aided and abetted by poor defense by the Dodgers – then held on to their advantage to beat the Dodgers, 6-5, in Game 3 of their National League Division Series.

The Padres lead the best-of-five series, two games to one, and will have a chance to close out the Dodgers at Petco Park for the second time in the past three Octobers.

"What's done is done now," Dodgers star Shohei Ohtani said through his interpreter. "So at this point it's really very simple. It's to win two games."

The Dodgers are 1-3 in their past four elimination games, having staved it off in Game 5 of the 2021 NL Championship Series before losing the next game. They will need back-to-back wins to advance out of this NLDS. They haven't won back-to-back postseason games since Games 4 and 5 of the 2021 NLDS against the San Francisco Giants.

"We can't look at the mountain. We have to just look at the task at hand and that's one pitch at a time," Mookie Betts said.

"It's going to be obviously a lot more pressure. Each at-bat is going to matter exponentially more, and so figure out a way to get it done."

Game 3 was fought on a razor's edge. The Dodgers made it a one-run game in the third inning with a grand slam by Teoscar Hernandez. But the Padres used their store-bought (through trade deadline acquisitions) bullpen to hold the Dodgers to just one baserunner over the final six innings.

"I liked how we fought," first baseman Freddie Freeman said. "We came back after that six-run inning. I know Dodger fans don't want to hear about fighting and stuff, but take the positive and come out here tomorrow."

The memory of Jurickson Profar's home run robbery in Game 2 still fresh in his mind, Betts couldn't believe his 0-for-22 postseason slump was over when he sent a fly ball into the left field seats in the first inning. Profar leaped and reached over the wall but this time the ball went off his glove and he came up empty.

Betts had peeled off near second base and was heading back to the dugout when third-base coach Dino Ebel and the umpires convinced Betts he really had hit a home run.

"The first game he kind of robbed it and acted like he didn't catch it, so I kind of thought it was the same thing," Betts said.

That sent Buehler to the mound with a 1-0 lead – making him the first Dodgers starting pitcher to take the mound with a lead at any point in a postseason game since Tyler Anderson in Game 4 of the 2022 NLDS against the Padres.

It didn't last. The Dodgers' defense collapsed around Buehler in the second inning.

After a Manny Machado single, Freeman went to his knees to stop Jackson Merrill's hard ground ball to his right. But he tried to throw from his knees and hit Machado in the back of his shoulder.

Machado was running on the infield grass when he was hit, and the Dodgers wanted an interference call.

"I mean, both feet are on the grass. I don't think that's part of the baseline," Buehler said. "But I'm not an umpire."

Dodgers manager Dave Roberts said there was nothing he could do because "it's not a replay-able challenge play."

"You can create your own base path if you're not avoiding a tag," Roberts said. "It was a heady play."

Freeman thought interference could have been called but admitted "I would have done the same thing as a base runner, to banana it" – meaning run wide to get into the throwing lane of the first baseman.

"But usually you're supposed to do it after one or two steps in the dirt and go," Freeman said. "I'm really far in the grass, and he got really far in the grass. … That's what we're taught as base runners, to get into the line, and he did it there."

Padres manager Mike Shildt echoed Roberts' understanding of the baserunning rule – "the base runner can create his own baseline until there's an actual attempted play on him," he said.

Fernando Tatis Jr. called it a "huge" moment in the game for the Padres.

"That's the highest IQ in baseball," Tatis said of Machado. "When you see plays like that … that's why Manny's Manny. This rally wouldn't have started probably if he hadn't made that play."

It wouldn't have happened without some more help from the Dodgers.

With runners at the corners now, Xander Bogaerts hit a slow ground ball near second base. Shortstop Miguel Rojas fielded it and made an uncharacteristically poor decision, trying to skip over to second base and turn a double play. He didn't get either out, and a run scored.

"That play has happened to me in my career a bunch of times and more times than not, I think 99 percent, today was the only time that I haven't gotten the runner at least at second base," Rojas said. "I felt like I was playing not all the way in the hole. I was playing in straight-up position and I was moving to my left already. I felt like the best way for us to get two outs there was that.

"But at the end of the day, you rethink about it and revisit the play, and all we needed was one out. I didn't know that the whole thing was going to happen after obviously, but getting one out there probably was the best option and I made a bad decision."

David Peralta followed with a two-run double. Kyle Higashioka drove in another run with a sacrifice fly and Tatis landed the big blow – a two-out, two-run home run.

Tatis' homer (his third in the past two games) was one of five balls Padres hitters put in play after Buehler got two strikes in the count. Buehler's inability to finish off hitters has been an issue throughout his comeback from Tommy John surgery.

"I'm not a 10, 11, 12 punchout per nine (innings) guy like I used to be," said Buehler, who didn't strike out anyone Tuesday. "I think going forward in my career, there's certainly some things that makes me feel like I can do that. But at this point in this year, I'm trying to get people to put the ball on the ground. And I felt pretty good about a lot of the things that I did. Obviously, the ones you're talking about, not a ton of them were hit 110 right? So, you know, they found spots and created momentum. I've talked ad nauseam about momentum in the playoffs, and I just couldn't make the one pitch to kind of stop it."

A Petco Park record crowd of 47,744 could be heard in Tijuana at that point and cameras caught Buehler venting his frustrations in the dugout, throwing his glove into the bench and giving a trash can a WWE-worthy body slam.

The therapy session worked. Buehler stayed in and put up zeroes over the next three innings.

And all the loud noises might have inspired the offense. Rojas, Ohtani and Betts led off the third inning with consecutive singles – although Rojas had to leave the game after aggravating the adductor strain he has been playing with.

After Freeman flew out, Hernandez got a hanging slider from Padres starter Michael King and sent it over the center field wall for a grand slam (only the sixth postseason grand slam in franchise history).

The next 16 Dodgers went down in order against King, Jeremiah Estrada, Jason Adam and Tanner Scott – who faced Ohtani for the third time in the three NLDS games in the eighth inning and struck him out for the third time.

Since his home run and single in Game 1, Ohtani has gone 1 for 10 with six strikeouts.

"Overall, I'm grateful that I'm even here, healthy and able to be in the postseason," Ohtani said. "So tomorrow I'm going to go out and do my best." ∎

NATIONAL LEAGUE DIVISION SERIES GAME 4
October 9, 2024 | San Diego, California
DODGERS 8, PADRES 0

What a Relief!

Eight Dodgers Pitchers Combine to Hold the Padres Scoreless, as the Offense Breaks Out

By Bill Plunkett

Like rescuers linking arms in a human chain to save someone in danger of drowning, the Dodgers' bullpen linked arms, ventured out on the thin ice of Game 4 and kept their season from going under.

Achieving peak 2024, the Dodgers resorted to a bullpen game in an elimination game. Eight pitchers wore a path from the bullpen to the mound at Petco Park on Wednesday night – then forced San Diego Padres hitters to wear a path back to their dugout.

Dodgers manager Dave Roberts stitched together a seven-hit shutout with those relievers and the Dodgers' offense piled up runs to stave off elimination with an 8-0 victory in Game 4 of their National League Division Series.

The Dodgers' two victories in this series have featured 15 scoreless innings from their relievers.

"We've said it all year. Our bullpen is special," said left-hander Alex Vesia (the fourth man up Wednesday). "We've got eight, nine, 10 guys that can all come in in very high-leverage situations and I think it shows. The script for us can be written in many different ways and we use that in our favor, big time."

If anyone thought resorting to a bullpen game with their backs to the wall was an off ramp to a last resort, they better think again, Vesia said.

"I would say they haven't watched enough Dodger baseball this year for them to be like that," he said. "I would say if they watched us they would have a different opinion."

Game 4 was the 25th bullpen game the Dodgers have used since the start of 2022 – they have won 17 of them. They became the second team ever to throw a nine-inning postseason shutout using at least eight pitchers.

"This isn't our first bullpen game," said Anthony Banda (second in the conga line). "It's understanding that the bullpen is a very important piece of this ballclub and there's a reason for that. I don't think that anybody deviated from what we've done in the regular season. I think everyone just went and laid it all out there because we knew what was at stake.

"We understood the assignment and we just continued to pass that baton on and understand we have that trust in the person coming in behind us."

Roberts' maneuvering wasn't even limited to the pitchers. He moved Kiké Hernandez and Chris Taylor between third base and center field. Hernandez went to center when fly ball pitchers like Michael Kopech and Alex Vesia were on the mound. Taylor went to center with Hernandez at third when ground balls were more likely.

This Surfliner Series heads back north for Game 5 at Dodger Stadium. The Dodgers have not taken a postseason series to the limit since beating the San Francisco Giants in five games in their 2021 NLDS – also the last time they won a postseason series.

Roberts would not name a starter for Game 5 on Wednesday, saying it could be Yoshinobu Yamamoto or

Mookie Betts got the Dodgers off on the right foot with a first-inning solo home run. (AP Images)

Jack Flaherty (who spent Game 4 in the bullpen in case "something funky happened").

"I think that we could run the same playbook back and run a bullpen game (in Game 5)," Roberts said.

Nothing funky happened in Game 4, and they handed the Padres their first shutout loss since July 19.

The Dodgers never trailed in the game thanks to the October rebirth of Mookie Betts, who homered in the first inning for the second consecutive game. This time, he didn't hit it anywhere near Jurickson Profar – and didn't hesitate going into an animated home run trot, pumping his fist as he rounded second base.

"I think we all knew Mookie was going to be Mookie," said Freddie Freeman, who sat out to rest his sprained ankle. "I know everyone wants to harp on certain things (like his 0-for-22 postseason slump), but he's Mookie Betts for a reason."

Two more runs in the second inning chased Padres right-hander Dylan Cease, who started on three days of rest but was pulled by Manager Mike Shildt after just five outs. Shohei Ohtani and Betts gave the Dodgers a 3-0 lead with back-to-back RBI singles – their largest lead at the end of a postseason inning since they led 5-0 midway through Game 1 of their 2022 NLDS against the Padres.

In the third inning, the Dodgers made it 5-0 on a 432-foot, two-run home run by Will Smith. It was the Dodgers' biggest lead at the end of a postseason inning since Game 1 of their 2022 NLDS against the Padres.

"I think it was huge. We got off to a hot start," Muncy said. "Especially in this place, this atmosphere. Kind of take a little bit of energy out of the crowd. It's really hard to do here. They still have a lot of energy. But just to take even a little bit out of it I think that was big for us and allowed our pitchers to go out there and execute their job and not have to stress about doing too much."

Ohtani cost them a chance to pad that lead with poor baserunning in the fourth inning. He drew a walk with one out then tagged up and went to second on a fly out by Betts. Teoscar Hernandez bounced a ground ball down the third-base line that Manny Machado tried to backhand as the ball bounced just across the foul line. It glanced off Machado's glove, bounced up and hit third-base umpire Mark Ripperger.

Third-base coach Dino Ebel threw up a stop sign when he saw the ball hit Ripperger, but Ohtani's head was down and he kept going. Machado was able to recover the ball quickly and threw Ohtani out at home.

The Dodgers' relievers were able to avoid any drama for most of the game. The Padres didn't have a baserunner with fewer than two outs until David Peralta led off the fifth inning with a single off Vesia.

Vesia walked Jake Cronenworth to put two runners on with no outs, but he struck out Kyle Higashioka and got Luis Arraez to fly out.

"For me, it's one pitch at a time. Try not to get too far ahead of myself. Execute. That's it," Vesia said. "Evan (Phillips) comes in behind me and gets a great out then has a super-efficient inning after me. That's my guy."

Phillips retired all four batters he was tasked with. By the time Daniel Hudson took the mound for the bottom of the seventh, the Dodgers had broken the game open with three more runs on a squeeze bunt by Tommy Edman and a two-run home run by Gavin Lux.

"We played a great game overall," Kiké Hernandez said. "We did a little bit of everything. We slugged, we rallied, went station to station. We bunted in some runs. And the offense had a great game.

"But we wouldn't have been in that position if it wasn't for the bullpen. So I think the bullpen were the players of the game tonight." ∎

Lefty Anthony Banda was one of eight Dodgers pitchers who combined to blank the Padres, 8-0. (AP Images)

NATIONAL LEAGUE DIVISION SERIES GAME 5

October 11, 2024 | Los Angeles, California

DODGERS 2, PADRES 0

'Job's Not Finished'

Eliminating the Padres is Just the First of Three Hurdles

By Mirjam Swanson

The day before the Dodgers' 2-0 victory in Game 5 of the National League Division Series, they had Kobe Bryant's quote posted on a screen in their clubhouse: "JOB'S NOT FINISHED."

You don't say, guys.

A scowling Bryant delivered that line in 2009 after the Lakers went up 2-0 in the NBA Finals, his commentary reflecting an acute and unflinching desire to win the grand prize, his unwillingness to even consider bending to complacency: "What's there to be happy about? Job's not finished."

The Dodgers were using it as a rallying cry after winning Game 4 to extend their NLDS and force a must-win Game 5. They had to win or they were finished for this season, two rounds shy of the World Series. It was win or let down their tormented fan base for the 11th time in 12 seasons. Obviously the job wasn't done.

And neither were the Dodgers, it turned out, finished.

Yoshinobu Yamamoto and a parade of fire-breathing relievers – Evan Phillips, Alex Vesia, Michael Kopech and Blake Treinen – kept the formidable Padres off the board, finishing them off with barely a whimper, scoreless in the final 24 innings of their 2024 season.

And at the plate, the Hernandezes – first Kiké and then Teoscar – gave the Dodgers all the offense they needed to advance past the NLDS for the first time since 2021, when they lost to the eventual champion Atlanta Braves in the NLCS, 4-2 … which is to say, they failed to finish the job.

It's been mission accomplished just once in this stretch of relative success, when they beat Tampa Bay in the strange confines of a 2020 COVID World Series and still hear about the asterisk some want to attach to a title won in a pandemic-shortened season.

Otherwise, the typically big-spending Dodgers – who came into this season with their largest payroll yet after committing $1.4 billion in future salaries to Shohei Ohtani and Yamamoto and others this past offseason – have been falling short of the grand prize.

And while, yes, the Dodgers finished with MLB's best regular-season record (98-64) for the fourth time in the past eight seasons – including the club-record 111 wins in 2022, when their season ended with a stunningly abrupt 3-1 NLDS loss to the Padres – it's not what the people really want.

The people don't want a pretty record or even a party so much as they want a parade.

"If there's something that this crowd is, it's hungry," said Kiké Hernandez before Friday's victory, in which he hit his 14th postseason home run, and sixth in a clinching game.

"They want a championship. They want another one. The one we had a couple years back, the city didn't get to celebrate it because of obvious circumstances. We know how bad they want it."

Blake Treinen rejoices after nailing down the save and helping the Dodgers clinch a berth in the NLCS. (Los Angeles Daily News: Keith Birmingham)

And so the job is still not finished. Far from it.

Even though the Dodgers danced on a champagne-logged clubhouse carpet while rapping along with Kendrick Lamar's mega-hit diss track "Not Like Us" after subduing their Southern California rivals, the work's not done.

"We won a series, we beat the Padres, and now we get to play the Mets," said Kiké Hernandez, in a statement that would have been most matter-of-fact if he hadn't been shouting it into a microphone while Miguel Rojas sprayed him in the face with champagne.

Said backward ballcap-sporting pitcher Jack Flaherty through the din: "We gotta refocus after this tonight, and move forward to the next."

But first, they celebrated getting over "a little bit of a DS funk," as Dodgers president of baseball operations Andrew Friedman called it. "For the guys who have been here, they could feel that after we got down 2-1, and the new guys wanted no part of that …"

So the Dodgers let loose as only baseball players will after moving past the divisional series for the first time in three tries.

And when they're finished celebrating having earned the right to host the New York Mets in Game 1 of the National League Championship Series on Sunday evening, they have a job to do.

These talented Ohtani-led Dodgers have two more series to win if they're going to live up to their potential (even with what amounts to a full pitching rotation sidelined by injury and Rojas and Freddie Freeman ailing, too).

They have work to do to disprove their doubters: "Eighty percent of the experts said we were gonna (freakin') lose, (forget) those guys, we know what we are!" infielder Max Muncy shouted amid the celebrating. "We were the (freaking) best team in baseball this year."

The (freaking) best team in baseball has got a job to finish if it's going to fulfill the fans' far-too-often deferred dreams. If it's going to celebrate not just as a playoff participant or divisional winner or National League pennant winner but, finally, as a World Series winner again. ∎

Kiké Hernandez ripped a solo home run in the second inning of Game 5, which would be all the Dodgers needed in the 2-0 shutout over the Padres. (Los Angeles Daily News: Keith Birmingham)

THIRD BASE/OUTFIELD

KIKÉ HERNANDEZ

Hernandez Once Again Demonstrates How He's Built for October

By Jeff Fletcher | October 11, 2024

When Kiké Hernandez blasted a home run that served as the first salvo in the Dodgers' National League Division Series-clinching victory, it was no surprise to Dave Roberts or anyone who has watched the October version of Hernandez in recent years.

"The reason we got him this year," the Dodgers manager said, "was to win 11 games in October."

Hernandez, 33, has played 11 years in the majors with a .238 batting average and a .713 OPS. Those rather pedestrian numbers pale in comparison to his .277 average and .899 OPS in 75 postseason games. His second-inning homer on a first-pitch fastball from Yu Darvish on Friday night was the 14th of his postseason career.

Hernandez hit three homers in the Dodgers' 2017 NL Championship Series clincher, and he hit five in 11 games for the 2021 Boston Red Sox.

"These are the games we've been dreaming of as kids," Hernandez said. "I got spoiled very early in my career to get the experience and get the opportunity to do this a lot. I think this is my ninth postseason now. It gets a little easier as you do it over and over again. It allows you to realize that it's the same game. The intensity and the importance of the game is a little – it gets a little enhanced.

"But I don't know, I don't know if it's because I'm Puerto Rican. I don't know what it is, but it just brings the best out of me and I'm glad that it does."

Roberts said the Dodgers can accept what he is in the regular season because they know what he can do in October.

"The focus every day (over 162 games) seems to be tougher for him," Roberts said. "But when you're talking about the biggest of stages, everyone knows Kiké, he loves the spotlight. And some people love it. Some people run from it.

"When you're talking about this market, the postseason, people in Puerto Rico watching him all over the country, that's when he's his best."

Hernandez left the Dodgers as a free agent following the pandemic-shortened 2020 season – just after helping them to win the World Series – and he returned in a midseason trade in 2023. Hernandez was a free agent again last winter, signing with the Dodgers after spring training began.

Roberts said it was a "bet" that he and the front office made to bring him back, figuring that he would come through at this time of year.

Kiké Hernandez is known to step his game up in the postseason, one of the main reasons the Dodgers brought him back for his second go round with the team. (Los Angeles Daily News: Keith Birmingham)

"When you talk about postseason in whatever sport, you can't be afraid to fail," Roberts said. "And this guy always rises to the occasion."

It wasn't always this way.

Hernandez was 4 for 21 in his first two postseasons with the Dodgers, in 2015 and 2016.

He said he took a new approach into 2017. He simply willed himself to success, visualizing big performances.

"It's very easy for you to see yourself failing in the postseason," Hernandez said. "And the anxiety, the self-doubt, all these things start creeping in your mind. … Whenever those thoughts come in, I visualize myself having success over and over again. You get to the field the next day and you have already seen the day happen. So nothing overwhelms over you, no moment gets too big."

And what did he visualize the night before this homer?

"Kind of that," he said. "But the bases were loaded." ■

Opposite: Kiké Hernandez's personality is a great fit for this Dodgers team, often seen having fun when he's not busy making huge plays in playoff games. (Los Angeles Daily News: David Crane) Above: Mookie Betts and Shohei Ohtani were ready to celebrate after Kiké Hernandez launched a go-ahead home run in Game 5 against the Padres. (Los Angeles Daily News: Keith Birmingham)

CHAMP

NLCS

NATIONAL LEAGUE CHAMPIONSHIP SERIES GAME 1
October 13, 2024 | Los Angeles, California
DODGERS 9, METS 0

Brothers in Arms

Dodgers Open NLCS with 3rd Consecutive Shutout

By Bill Plunkett

New Yorkers like to complain about how difficult it is to find a good bagel outside of the city. The Dodgers gave them nine to choose from Sunday night.

Picking up right where they left off in their series with the San Diego Padres, the Dodgers continued their scoreless streak with a third consecutive shutout, beating the New York Mets, 9-0, in Game 1 of their National League Championship Series.

"Our pitchers have been amazing," outfielder Mookie Betts said accurately.

It's a historic run of dominance. The Dodgers have not given up a run since the second inning of Game 3 in the NL Division Series. The 33 consecutive scoreless innings by Dodgers pitchers is tied for the longest streak in postseason history with the Baltimore Orioles, who shut out the Dodgers for 33 consecutive innings during the 1966 World Series.

The Dodgers have scored 23 unanswered runs while holding the Padres and Mets to zeroes during the scoreless streak. Dodgers pitchers have held the opposing hitters to a .127 average (14 for 110) during the streak.

"I think it's just a collective effort," Dodgers manager Dave Roberts said. "Certainly the players that were involved in all those scoreless innings have been fantastic. Defensively, we've been very good, converting outs when we need to. I think the coaches have done a great job of relaying the information and making it tangible and allowing for our pitchers and catchers to do a great job of sequencing.

"And the front office, just the information we get. I just think that how we're preventing runs, it's a complete team effort, collective effort."

The bullpen carried more of the load in back-to-back shutouts to end the NLDS. But it was a starter – they still have those in baseball these days – who kept it going Sunday.

Jack Flaherty retired the first nine Mets in order, didn't give up a hit until the fifth inning or a run in seven innings and became the first Dodgers starter to touch the mound in the seventh inning of a postseason start since Max Scherzer in Game 3 of their 2021 NLDS against the San Francisco Giants – 20 postseason games ago.

"It was just a pitching clinic," Roberts said. "I thought he did a great job of filling up the strike zone with his complete (pitch) mix. Used his fastball when he needed to. … And once we caught a lead, he did a great job of just going after those guys and attacking."

The Mets made Flaherty sweat just once – and then bungled their way out of a scoring opportunity in a callback to their franchise origins.

Jesse Winker led off the fifth inning with a single and Jose Iglesias dumped another into shallow left-center field. Winker got a good jump and rounded second base, heading for third base. Center fielder Kiké Hernandez fielded the ball and set up to throw to third base. Winker

Mookie Betts (left) and Freddie Freeman embrace at home plate after scoring on Max Muncy's RBI single in the first inning of Game 1. (Los Angeles Daily News: Keith Birmingham)

saw that and froze. When Hernandez threw across his body to second base instead, Winker was caught in no-man's land and thrown out.

The next two Mets flew out to end the threat.

"It was a huge play," Roberts said. "The game was still in the balance, and they started to kind of build an inning.

"But Kiké's heads-up kind of look – body going towards third and then throw behind the runner – just a heady baseball play. And that right there I thought took the wind out of their sail."

Having faced down the best team they are likely to face this postseason in the NLDS, Roberts said before the game he wanted his team to "push on" and not "let down your guard or get off the gas."

Kodai Senga made it easy for them.

The Mets' starting pitcher made just one start during the regular season due to shoulder and calf injuries and was limited in how many pitches he would be able to throw in a postseason start. He burned up 23 of them in the first inning, walking three consecutive batters to load the bases with one out. After Will Smith flew out and the runners held, Max Muncy came through with a two-out, two-run single.

"I thought you could see clearly that Senga just didn't have his 'A' stuff tonight," Roberts said. "The split was non-competitive. He didn't use his sweeper. And then he was just relying on the cutter, working behind hitters, walking guys."

Senga walked the first batter he faced in the second inning as well. After Tommy Edman bunted him to second, Shohei Ohtani drove in the Dodgers' third run with a single.

That was it for Senga, who threw just 10 strikes in his 30 pitches. The Dodgers did nothing to help him. Of his 20 pitches outside the strike zone, Dodgers hitters swung at just two – one cutter and one slider.

"We wanted to get Senga out of the game early," first baseman Freddie Freeman said. "We knew his pitch count was not going to be that high. Get to their bullpen, kind of create some havoc for them later on in the series."

While Flaherty was breezing through the Mets' lineup, the Dodgers doubled their lead with a three-run fourth inning.

Kiké Hernandez led off with a single and moved up on their second sacrifice bunt of the game, this one by Gavin Lux. Edman cashed it in with an RBI single and Ohtani followed with a 116.5 mph laser off the wall in right-center field. When Starling Marte bobbled the ball, Edman scored from first and Ohtani moved to second. Freeman drove him in with another two-out hit.

In the first postseason of his MLB career, Ohtani has built an odd stat line – he is 6 for 8 with runners on base, 0 for 16 when he bats with the bases empty.

The bases were loaded after Ohtani walked in the eighth inning, then Betts drove in three runs with a double.

"I think after an intense series like the last one where you play with a lot of energy, we were aware that you can definitely fall into a little lull and come out flat," Edman said. "So we really made it a priority to come out with that energy and really take it to them and we did a great job of that in the first few innings. Kept the momentum up.

"Come out with the same energy and get after them again tomorrow."

The Dodgers will try to break their tie with the Orioles by going with a bullpen game in Game 2.

"Thirty-three scoreless innings in a row now? It's been unbelievable," Lux said. "And against playoff lineups that have really good hitters in them. They (the bullpen) have been horses for us all year." ∎

Shohei Ohtani celebrates after scoring on Freddie Freeman's RBI single to give the Dodgers a 5-0 lead in the fourth inning of Game 1. (Los Angeles Daily News: Keith Birmingham)

NATIONAL LEAGUE CHAMPIONSHIP SERIES GAME 2
October 14, 2024 | Los Angeles, California
METS 7, DODGERS 3

Even the Score

Resilient Mets Punch Back at Dodgers, Head Home with NLCS Tied

By Jeff Fletcher

Surely you didn't expect the New York Mets to go down quite as easily as they did in Game 1.

A day after the Dodgers blew out the Mets by nine runs, Grimace's favorite team evened the National League Championship Series by showing what helped them flip the switch from an awful start to an electric finish this season.

"We get punched in the face, and we continue to find ways to get back up," Mets manager Carlos Mendoza said after their 7-3 victory in Game 2. "And it will continue to be that way."

In case you missed the rollercoaster of their season, the Mets were off to a terrible start, falling 11 games under .500. They turned their season around with a seven-game winning streak – starting when McDonalds' iconic purple monster threw out a first pitch in June. That began a stretch in which the Mets went 60-36, the best record in the majors over that span.

Since then, they dispatched two of the National League's division winners – the Milwaukee Brewers and Philadelphia Phillies – in the playoffs, and now they have their sights set on the third.

It wasn't looking so good when the Dodgers thumped the Mets, 9-0, in the opener, running their scoreless innings streak to 33.

That streak didn't even last one batter into Game 2.

Francisco Lindor – the likely runner-up to Shohei Ohtani for NL MVP – led off the game with a homer.

Lindor had blasted a go-ahead homer in the game that put the Mets into the playoffs, and he also drilled a grand slam to give the Mets the lead in the division series clincher against the Phillies.

Lindor has been so good in the clutch for the Mets that no one batted an eye when the Dodgers intentionally walked him to load the bases in the second inning.

Third baseman Mark Vientos, who was on deck, certainly knows intellectually that it's the right baseball move to pitch to him instead of Lindor.

Still …

"For sure, I took it personal," Vientos said. "I want to be up there during that at-bat for sure. I want them to walk Lindor in that situation, put me up there. And at that point I was just, let me simplify the game, just get one run in, get a walk – whatever I can do to add another run to the score. And luckily I hit a bomb there and it went over the fence."

Vientos hit a grand slam that extended the Mets' lead to 6-0.

Although they didn't finish off the blowout with the same efficiency as the Dodgers had the night before – the Mets' defense was shaky and they walked eight – they nonetheless got the victory.

Now, the teams will head across the country and play three straight games at Citi Field, where the Mets' fans just cheered their team on to back-to-back victories to vanquish the Phillies.

"I expect it to be crazy," said Mets left-hander Sean Manaea, who picked up the victory on Monday. "Last time we were there playing the Phillies, it was wild. I expect nothing less. Just very excited to be back there."

Getting a split in the first two games of a best-of-seven series is always the road team's goal, because it changes the series into a best-of-five with the next three at home.

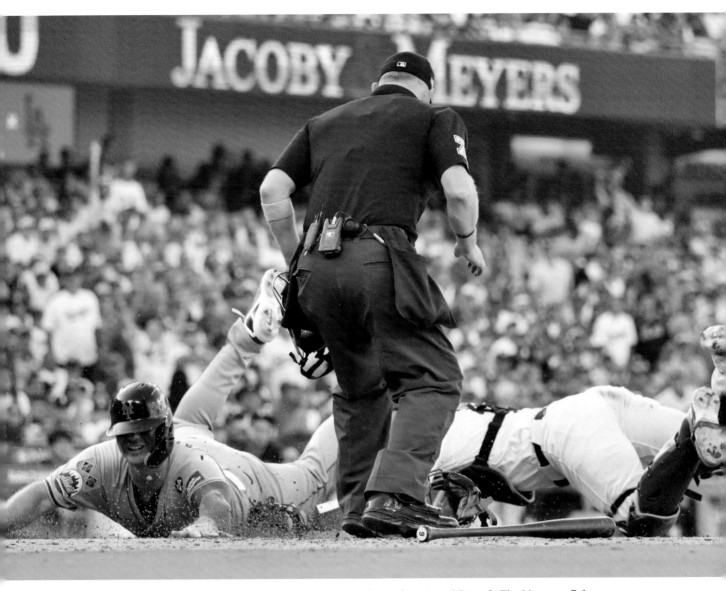

Pete Alonso slides past the reach of Dodgers catcher Will Smith in the ninth inning of Game 2. The Mets won 7-3 to even the series. (Los Angeles Daily News: Keith Birmingham)

"We've got a chance to take the series at home," Mets closer Edwin Diaz said. "So I feel really good. We are really happy. We played a really good game today. Just continue what we're doing and we will be fine."

The Mets, of course, are aware that the momentum they gained by winning Game 2 will vanish if they don't win Game 3. They know that the Dodgers are just as capable of bouncing back from a tough loss as they were.

"It's a seven-game series; it's not a sprint," Manaea said. "It's definitely going to be a grind of a series. Those guys over there are going to do the same. Just come in and each day and take it as it is, and go out there and play baseball like we know how to." ■

NATIONAL LEAGUE CHAMPIONSHIP SERIES GAME 3
October 16, 2024 | New York, New York
DODGERS 8, METS 0

Built for the Moment

Max Muncy, Kiké Hernandez and Shohei Ohtani Hit Home Runs in 8-0 Win

By Bill Plunkett

The Dodgers are putting the O's in OMG.

For the second time in the first three games of this National League Championship Series and the fourth time in their past five games this postseason the Dodgers used a group effort to spin a shutout and beat the New York Mets, 8-0, in Game 3 on Wednesday night at Citi Field.

The Mets – who have used infielder Jose Iglesias' Latin pop hit "OMG" as their theme song as they salvaged their season – managed just four hits. Max Muncy alone was on base more than that – not for long the last time. After three walks and a single, Muncy joined Kiké Hernandez and Shohei Ohtani in hitting home runs.

The win puts the Dodgers up two games to one in the best-of-seven NLCS.

"To have the advantage in the playoff series is huge," starting pitcher Walker Buehler said. "I always talk about momentum in the playoffs, whether it's an inning or a game or a series. And this is definitely a big momentum win for us. But if we don't do something with it, then it doesn't really matter a whole lot."

Buehler got that momentum started with four stress-filled scoreless innings.

"Walker was Walker Buehler. It's what we expected. It's what everyone in this clubhouse trusted him to be,"

Muncy said. "He thrives in these moments. There's never a moment that gets too big for him. There's never a situation that gets too big for him. He's able to control everything. He was Walker Buehler tonight."

He was. But only by the postseason's lowering bar for starting pitchers. The Mets had runners on base in each of the first three innings, loading the bases in the second – and got nothing to show for it.

Buehler struck out Pete Alonso with a runner on in the first inning. After two walks and a misplayed grounder by shortstop Tommy Edman loaded the bases with one out in the second, Buehler got a called third strike on Francisco Alvarez then dropped a full-count hammer of a curveball on Francisco Lindor to escape damage.

"Oh, in 2018, 2019, 2020, I would have thrown a fastball. Yeah," Buehler said, acknowledging the metamorphosis he is undergoing since returning from his second elbow surgery.

"That with 3-2 and the bases loaded, I have to throw a curveball now instead of a heater," he said of the most difficult lesson he has learned in his comeback season.

But that curveball might have been the most important pitch of the night.

"That was great," Muncy said. "I don't think anyone over there would have expected Walker to throw that pitch in that situation and that's why Walker did it. He

Kiké Hernandez homers in the sixth inning of Game 3 to give the Dodgers a 4-0 lead. It was his 15th home run in 78 career postseason games. (AP Images)

executed it and that's what he does. He showed the emotion there and got us all fired up for sure."

It was more of the same in the third after the Mets put two on with two outs. Buehler struck out Mets DH J.D. Martinez with a sweeper breaking off the plate.

Buehler struck out six in the first four innings and got a season-high 18 swings-and-misses – six each on his curveball and sweeper.

It was vintage Buehler in those moments. But Dodgers manager Dave Roberts was still guarding against the more recent vintage. With the high-leverage core of the Dodgers' bullpen well-rested, Roberts had no plans to let Buehler face the Mets' lineup a third time.

If Buehler's four innings were difficult, Luis Severino's were no less torturous. The two Game 3 starters combined for 8⅔ innings – and most of FOX's broadcast hours for the week. Buehler and Severino threw 185 pitches to get less than halfway through the game. At least Buehler was able to avoid damage. Severino could not.

Muncy drew the first of his three walks in the game leading off the second inning. Teoscar Hernandez chopped a ball in front of the plate that catcher Alvarez fielded and thought he could get the lead runner. His throw was wide of second base and the Dodgers had two on with no outs.

After Gavin Lux grounded out to the pitcher, Will Smith hit another one back to the mound. Severino – a finalist for a Gold Glove this season – couldn't field this one and a run scored. Tommy Edman hit the only well-struck ball of the inning – a fly ball that center fielder Tyrone Taylor tracked down on the warning track, making an outstanding catch. A second run scored on the sacrifice fly, the only ball that left the infield all inning.

Balls started leaving the infield with more frequency against the Mets' bullpen. Kiké Hernandez doubled the Dodgers' lead with a two-run home run in the sixth inning, his second homer this postseason and 15th in 78 career postseason games.

"He's got it. Whatever it is, he's got it," Smith said of Hernandez's ability to step up in the postseason.

Shohei Ohtani definitely has "it" during the regular season. But he has yet to establish that in the postseason. He didn't bat with runners on base in Game 3 until the eighth inning – and launched a three-run home run into the right field upper deck.

"Obviously you ask the umpires to take a look because it doesn't cost you a challenge," Muncy said of the replay review that followed. "But I don't know how you ever overturn it. That ball was 100 feet over the foul pole. The foul pole's not tall enough for that one."

Ohtani is now an amazing 7 for 9 with two home runs with runners on base in his first eight postseason games – and a mystifying 0 for 22 with 13 strikeouts when no one is on base.

With the score still tight, Roberts ran with Michael Kopech in the fifth inning, Ryan Brasier in the sixth and Blake Treinen in the seventh. With the game tilted to 7-0 in the Dodgers' favor by Ohtani's blast, he closed with Ben Casparius over the final two scoreless innings, saving Evan Phillips and Daniel Hudson for another day.

"They're good. We have some good pitchers," Muncy said of the Dodgers' four shutouts. "I think the biggest thing is we have good attitudes in terms of how to handle the postseason atmosphere. We've got a lot of guys that are built for the moment and you've seen it." ∎

Max Muncy celebrates with Shohei Ohtani after Muncy's home run to lead off the ninth inning of Game 3. Muncy reached base in each of his five at-bats in Game 3. (AP Images)

NATIONAL LEAGUE CHAMPIONSHIP SERIES GAME 4

October 17, 2024 | New York, New York

DODGERS 10, METS 2

Walk the Walk

Betts and Ohtani Lead Dodgers to Game 4 Victory, One Win from World Series

By Bill Plunkett

The Dodgers are about to turn the New York Mets into playoff pumpkins.

Mookie Betts had four hits and drove in four runs and Shohei Ohtani scored four times as the Dodgers beat the Mets, 10-2, in Game 4 of the National League Championship Series to move within one win of returning to the World Series.

Up three games to one now, the Dodgers will try to close out the Mets and reach the 22nd World Series in franchise history (the fourth in the past eight years) in Game 5 on Friday.

"Obviously it'd be huge (to close out the series on Friday)," infielder Max Muncy said. "But our mindset is it's a 0-0 series. We've got to go out there and play it the right way, do things the right way, and that's what we're planning on."

The Dodgers are set to chase the Mets out of the postseason because they have been unwilling to chase. In the four NLCS games, the Dodgers have drawn 31 walks against Mets pitchers. According to statistician Sarah Langs, that is the most for a four-game span at any point in a postseason.

Twelve of those walks became runs – the Mets have scored a total of only nine runs in the series.

It's the IRL implementation of the Dodgers' pre-postseason game-planning sessions where it was emphasized that the most successful teams in the postseason are usually the ones that are most disciplined at the plate.

"There was definitely some talks about it," Muncy said. "But I think the biggest thing was understanding more in-depth why that is. And it's being aggressive on balls in the zone. Not taking balls in the zone. And not swinging out of the zone. And I think that's just a deeper understanding for us, understanding who we are as a team, and what certain pitches we can hit, what pitches we can't hit. And we've had an entire lineup being able to buy into that."

No one has been more disciplined than Muncy. He walked in each of his first three times up in Game 4 then singled in the seventh inning, extending a streak of reaching base to 12 consecutive plate appearances – eight walks, two singles and two home runs – before he struck out in the eighth inning.

That is a record for a single postseason and ties Reggie Jackson for the overall postseason record. Jackson's streak of 12 stretched from the 1977 postseason into 1978.

Shohei Ohtani led off the game with a home run – his third homer of the postseason and second of the NLCS and his first hit with nobody on base. Mark Vientos matched that for the Mets in the bottom of the first off Yoshinobu Yamamoto.

But the Dodgers didn't give in to Mets starter Jose Quintana and started cashing in their free passes in the third inning.

"We knew Quintana – I think he had the lowest percentage in-zone as a starting pitcher. That was what

Mookie Betts celebrates after hitting a two-run home run in the sixth inning of Game 4. Betts had four hits and four RBIs in the Dodgers' 10-2 win (AP Images)

we talked about in the hitters' meeting," said All-Star first baseman Freddie Freeman, who sat out Game 4, nursing his injured ankle. "The thing is, when you have plans and you stick to them, most of the time they're going to work out.

"We had a plan tonight: Don't give in to the nibble with Quintana. Make him keep the ball over the plate, and they did a great job."

After his first-inning home run, Ohtani didn't get much to hit and didn't force the issue. He walked in his next three times up and came around to score each time.

"There was a stretch there for, like, two or three at-bats I don't think he even saw a pitch remotely close, which I understand," Betts said. "But it's going to be tough to just walk him all the time.

"We'll see. If they want to continue to do it, that's okay. I just need to make sure I take care of my job and the guys behind us."

Betts did his job in Game 4. He and Ohtani were on base eight times and scored seven runs.

"I think he took it the same way (Mark) Vientos took it – personal," Dodgers manager Dave Roberts said of Betts watching the Mets' cautious approach to Ohtani. "That's okay. And I think that he understands that whether it's a manager putting four fingers up or you're throwing intentional balls two feet outside, you're going to go after the next guy.

"So I think that Mookie takes it personal like all competitors should. And I do think that stuff lights a little fire under him."

The first of Ohtani's walks came in the third inning. Betts followed with a single. Tommy Edman drove Ohtani in with a double and Kiké Hernandez sent Betts home with an infield single, shortstop Francisco Lindor smothering the ground ball to save another run.

The Dodgers were back at it in the fourth inning. Chris Taylor beat out an infield single and Ohtani walked again to put two runners on with one out for Betts. He lashed a double into the left-field corner, strutting as he

reached second base and two runs scored for the Dodgers.

Two innings later, Ohtani walked again and scored his fourth run of the game when Betts launched a hanging slider from Mets reliever Phil Maton into the left field seats.

That put the Dodgers ahead 7-2 with rested high-leverage relievers to close it out.

But things got dicey for the Dodgers in the sixth.

Evan Phillips (pitching for the first time since Game 5 of the NL Division Series) got the final two outs of the fifth inning in relief of Yamamoto. When he went back out for the sixth, he gave up back-to-back singles and walked J.D. Martinez to load the bases with no outs.

Phillips started to back away from the stove by striking out Jose Iglesias. He got Jeff McNeil to line out to center field, shallow enough for the runners to hold. Blake Treinen came in and finished it off, stranding all three runners when Jesse Winker lined out to right.

The Dodgers took the leverage from high to low with a three-run eighth inning highlighted by a two-run double from Edman.

"You've got to give them credit because that's a really good lineup and they can do a lot of different things," Mets manager Carlos Mendoza said. "This is a team that controls the strike zone as well as anybody in the league. Not only do they do that, but when they force you in the zone they can do some damage. And they've done that. They did it again today. They controlled the strike zone. They forced Quintana to come in on the strike zone. And when he did, they made him pay." ∎

Shohei Ohtani led off Game 4 with a home run, walked three times and scored four runs in the Dodgers' win. (AP Images)

NATIONAL LEAGUE CHAMPIONSHIP SERIES GAME 5

October 18, 2024 | New York, New York

METS 12, DODGERS 6

'We'll Be Ready'

Mets Rough Up Jack Flaherty in Game 5 to extend NLCS

By Bill Plunkett

Put a cork in it.

The tarp taped above the lockers in the visitors' clubhouse at Citi Field was never put to use. The champagne stayed on ice. Whatever visions the Dodgers might have had about closing out the New York Mets in five games and celebrating Friday night had to be stored away in the overhead space for the flight back to Los Angeles.

So dominant in the series opener, Jack Flaherty was not the same pitcher in Game 5. The Mets scored eight times in the first three innings, putting the Dodgers so far in a hole that even two home runs from Andy Pages and one from Mookie Betts couldn't dig them out. The Mets extended the National League Championship Series to a sixth game with a 12-6 victory.

The Dodgers still hold the advantage, 3-2, in the best-of-seven series. But now they will try to close it out with a bullpen game – the omnipresent pumpkin spice of the 2024 postseason – in Game 6 at Dodger Stadium.

"We lost. We can't go cry. It is what it is," Betts said. "Got to turn the page and get ready for the next one.

"We have to win one game in a couple days. Got to focus up and take care of business."

This series is still looking for its first close game. The Dodgers rolled into Game 5 with a plus-21 run differential – the highest through four games of a series in postseason history. Only one of the first four games was decided by less than eight runs (the Mets' 7-3 victory in Game 2).

The Mets did their best to keep that tilted theme going against Flaherty.

The Dodgers right-hander allowed just two hits in seven scoreless innings in Game 1. But his fastball velocity was down this time. He averaged 91.2 mph on his 26 four-seam fastballs, down 2 mph from his season average. He couldn't find the strike zone consistently with anything and when he did the Mets hit it hard – nine balls with exit velocities of 98 mph or higher.

"He wasn't sharp, clearly," Dodgers manager Dave Roberts said. "He's been fighting something. He's been under the weather a little bit. So I don't know if that bled into the stuff, the velocity. I'm not sure."

Pete Alonso landed the first big blow, a three-run home run in the first inning after the Dodgers wasted a scoring opportunity in the top of the inning.

A single by Shohei Ohtani and a double by Mookie Betts (when right fielder Starling Marte butchered his slicing line drive) put runners at second and third with no outs. But Ohtani held at third when Teoscar Hernandez grounded out to shortstop – during the FOX in-game interview Roberts called it "a brain cramp." Freddie Freeman lined out and Tommy Edman struck out and the Dodgers came away with nothing.

Flaherty stranded a runner at third in the second inning, but the Mets beat him up in the third inning as Roberts sat on his hands, opting against a quick hook to keep the game close.

"Those are thoughts that went through my head. But I think for me, I have five leverage guys that I wanted to make sure that you gotta deploy at the right time," Roberts explained.

"It's not always fun when you're going through it, certainly from anyone's chair, certainly my chair. But you have to kind of remain steadfast in how you use your pitchers because ultimately it's about winning four

Dodgers right fielder Mookie Betts chases down Jesse Winker's single in the eighth inning of Game 5, one of the Mets' 14 hits in a 12-6 trouncing of the Dodgers to avoid elimination. (AP Images)

games in a seven-game series."

The Mets sent nine batters to the plate in the inning. Flaherty walked the first two batters and gave up four hits, including a two-run double to Starling Marte, RBI singles to Francisco Alvarez and Brandon Nimmo and an RBI triple by Francisco Lindor.

"We didn't chase his secondary pitches," Mets manager Carlos Mendoza said. "We know he's got that slider and the knuckle curve, and he's going to try to make us chase and we didn't do that today. And when he came in the zone with his fastball, we were ready, and that's the key."

Flaherty credited the Mets for making the adjustments from Game 1 "and I didn't."

"Part of the challenge of it and what makes the postseason so interesting is facing the same team in the span of five days and getting a chance to go right back at them," Flaherty said. "I know they want to get back for what went on in Game 1. I wanted to keep rolling through that. That's not the way it went. They did a good job.

"If I could take the ball in the next game I would. But that's not the way that baseball works. Honey did a good job picking us up, giving us some innings. The guys kept showing up to fight, putting up six runs there. That makes it sting a little bit more because all I have to do is be average and we're in this game."

At 8-2, Roberts pulled Flaherty and went to Brent Honeywell Jr., marshaling his relief resources for Game 6. Honeywell had given the Dodgers three scoreless innings in a similar save-the-pen situation in Game 2. Like Flaherty, he couldn't reprise his success.

Honeywell gave up four runs in 4⅔ innings – the longest outing of his major-league career – before Roberts pulled him with two outs in the bottom of the eighth.

"I tried to keep us in the game," Honeywell said. "We had a shot to win the game, I felt like. We made the turn a little bit. Battled our ass off here. We knew they were gonna fight tonight. That's playoff baseball. Once you get in, save the dogs."

The Mets' continued scoring negated the Dodgers' attempts at a comeback. Pages hit a solo home run in the fourth inning and a three-run homer in the fifth. Betts led off the sixth with a solo shot. But the Dodgers had just one infield hit the rest of the way.

"Off day (Saturday) then we're back at home in front of our fans and the place will be rocking," Max Muncy said. "We'll have our staff ready to go and we'll be ready." ∎

RIGHT FIELDER/SHORTSTOP

MOOKIE BETTS

Dodgers' All-Star Turned Around Postseason Slump with Hard Work

By Bill Plunkett | October 21, 2024

Mookie Betts has a simple philosophy about hitting.

"Can't find it if you're not looking," he says.

For Betts, that search means taking hundreds of swings a day when he feels he's not contributing the way he should. At various times this postseason – which began with him mired in an 0-for-22 postseason slump that weighed heavily on his mind – he has referred to taking anywhere from "a couple hundred swings a day" to 500 swings in one day.

Do the math.

A conservative pace during a normal batting practice session would be five swings per minute. To get to 500 swings then would take 100 minutes. That kind of workout can tax the hands, the forearms, the legs – and the mind.

"No, that came from me," Betts said when asked if someone had suggested his carpet bombing approach to addressing any dissatisfaction with his swing. "Nobody recommends that."

Betts' good friend and hitting mentor, Mets designated hitter J.D. Martinez, is legendary for the hours he spends in the batting cage daily. But Martinez said his standard approach would be to take four or five swings then step out of the cage and review his swings on a tablet before stepping back in.

There are times when he does that, too, Betts said – but sometimes it is a high-volume search for answers.

"It just depends on where I'm at, what day it is, what we're working on," he said. "There's not necessarily a method. It's just madness in there.

"That's what I know. I work."

The madness has worked. Betts said he has continued to take hundreds of swings each day during the postseason – "probably taking way too many, but I'd rather do that."

"If I'm not hitting, I'm thinking about hitting," he said. "So I might as well be in the cage."

Since breaking his 0-for-22 postseason slide, Betts has gone 12 for 34 (.353) with four home runs in the past eight games, making this one of the best postseason performances of his career.

"Amazing," fellow outfielder Teoscar Hernandez said of watching Betts' work ethic. "You learn a lot from a guy that's won MVPs, World Series. All the awards that you can think about in baseball, he has it. He's just Mookie. He does special things."

In the first half of the season, Betts took a similar approach to learning how to play shortstop. He spent

Mookie Betts hit .289 with 19 home runs in his fifth season as a Dodger in 2024.
(Los Angeles Daily News: Keith Birmingham)

extra hours on the field long before game time, taking ground balls the way he takes swings in the cage, trying to accumulate the experience at the position he lacked.

The question then was the same – wasn't he worried about overdoing it?

"I don't care about overdoing it. I'd rather overdo it than not give effort," he says now of his hitting work. "Pretty much as soon as I get to the park I'm in the cage and I don't leave until I go back on the field. And I come back inside and I hit some more. That's what I've been doing."

He is also not worried about the extra work wearing down his 5-foot-9, 170-pound body. At 32, he said he takes care of his body better than he ever has. He begins each day with a yoga-like stretching and flexibility program that he adopted this spring after working with Osamu Yada – the personal trainer known as 'Yada Sensei' who works with Yoshinobu Yamamoto, creating much of his unique workout regimen featuring wooden blocks, weighted soccer balls and lawn dart-esque javelins.

"Especially in a time like now, there's not very many tomorrows. They run out pretty quick," Betts said. "So I'm really just trying to do what I can to help us, and the last thing I want to do is not give it 100, 110 percent.

"It's not something that I want to do. I don't want to go in there and hit all day. But it's something that, based off of my play, I need to do." ∎

Mookie Betts fields a ground ball at shortstop during a May 22 game against the Arizona Diamondbacks. Betts took on a new position in 2024, playing 65 games at shortstop. (Los Angeles Daily News: Keith Birmingham)

NATIONAL LEAGUE CHAMPIONSHIP SERIES GAME 6

October 20, 2024 | Los Angeles, California

DODGERS 10, METS 5

World Series or Bust!

Dodgers Beat Mets in Game 6, Head to World Series Reunion with Yankees

By Bill Plunkett

Every year, the Dodgers drive out of spring training as a high-priced luxury vehicle with a 'World Series or bust' bumper sticker. They swerved around more potholes than usual this season and dropped a few parts along the way.

But all the miles have led them to their destination this time – where they find another high-priced luxury vehicle with its own weathered 'World Series or bust' bumper sticker waiting to race them for more than pink slips.

Getting four RBIs from National League Championship Series MVP Tommy Edman, a two-run home run from Will Smith and plenty more in support of the latest collective effort from their bullpen, the Dodgers punched their ticket to the World Series with a 10-5 victory over the New York Mets in Game 6 of the NLCS.

The Dodgers fell behind two games to one in their NL Division Series against the Padres, raising the specter of their first-round exits in 2022 and 2023. Since then, they have won six of eight games.

"I think they proved to themselves how tough they are," said Dodgers manager Dave Roberts, who matched Bruce Bochy for the most World Series appearances (four) among active managers. "I think that when you get in a position that we were in against a division rival, against a very talented team at that point, it turns into a street fight. And it's lose and go home or you just fight like heck. And I think that that's what got us over the top

in the DS and also what bled into the fact it allowed us to finish these guys off in six games."

The Dodgers are heading to the World Series for the 22nd time in franchise history, the fourth time in the past eight years – but the first time since their pandemic 'bubble' championship in 2020. They will face their ancient nemesis, the New York Yankees, for the 12th time in the World Series, the first time since 1981. Game 1 is at Dodger Stadium.

"As a fan of baseball, how could you not be excited about this?" Dodgers infielder Max Muncy said, getting the hype train rolling. "You're talking about two of the biggest franchises. The biggest stars in the sport. You've got Freddie, Mookie, Shohei. On the other side you've got Aaron Judge, Giancarlo, Juan Soto, Gerrit Cole. The game's biggest stars on the biggest stage – how can you not be excited about this as a fan?

"Come on, man. It's Dodgers-Yankees – come on!"

With a pitching staff depleted by injuries, the Dodgers knew they were going to have to hit their way to this World Series. So they did. They outscored the Mets 46-26 in the NLCS with eight runs or more in four of the six games. The 46 runs are a franchise record for any postseason series and a National League record for an LCS.

Just as they did in 2020, the Dodgers rode a slugging shortstop to their NLCS victory. An unexpected star, Edman's 11 RBIs in the six games against the Mets matched the Dodgers' postseason record set by Corey

Reliever Blake Treinen celebrates with catcher Will Smith and teammates after recording the last out of the Dodgers' clinching Game 6 win over the Mets. (Los Angeles Daily News: Keith Birmingham)

Seager during their seven-game NLCS victory over the Atlanta Braves in 2020.

"We had really good at-bats throughout the series," Edman said, unaware that he had matched a record until after the game. "Our whole lineup was a really good lineup. Any number of guys could have won MVP.

"I kept getting up with guys on base and had a lot of opportunities to drive runs in."

Edman's season was put on hold by offseason wrist surgery and an ankle injury suffered during his rehab. He didn't play his first game until mid-August – after the Dodgers traded for him even though he was on the St. Louis Cardinals' injured list.

That late start gave Edman his own personal calendar. For him, he said earlier this week, it feels like his season has reached May or maybe June.

Call him Mr. June then. Edman went 11 for 27 in the NLCS with three doubles, a home run and those 11 RBIs.

"When we got him, we said 'NLCS MVP or bust.' So fortunately we don't bust," Dodgers president of baseball operations Andrew Friedman joked.

Edman moved from center field to shortstop when Miguel Rojas was left off the NLCS roster. And he moved to cleanup twice this series with All-Star first baseman Freddie Freeman on the bench with his injured ankle.

He started the scoring in the first inning driving in two runs with a double into the left field corner. That offset an early 1-0 lead ceded by Michael Kopech in the top of the inning. Deployed as the opener by the Dodgers, Kopech did everything but hit the bull with a pitch during the first inning. He walked two, threw a wild pitch and gave up a run when Chris Taylor made a throw wide of first base on Pete Alonso's broken-bat grenade on the infield.

Edman's double provided the first – and only – lead change of the entire series.

The Dodger relievers didn't have to be perfect the way it was when the team resorted to a bullpen game in

an elimination scenario (Game 4 of the Division Series against the San Diego Padres).

And they weren't. The Mets had 18 baserunners – 11 hits, six walks and a hit batter. They had more than one baserunner in six of the first seven innings.

Two-run home runs from Edman and Smith in the third inning made it a 6-1 lead. But Anthony Banda surrendered a two-run home run of his own, to Mark Vientos, tightening things up. Evan Phillips loaded the bases in the sixth but escaped without allowing a run.

Blake Treinen (the Dodgers' seventh and final pitcher of the night) took over in the eighth and put an end to the Mets' dreams of a miracle. He struck out the side in the eighth.

The Dodgers gave him three more runs in the bottom of the inning. Treinen gave one back before converting the first save opportunity for either team in this series.

Moments later, Roberts was raising the National League championship trophy and asking a roaring Dodger Stadium crowd "You guys want a parade in Los Angeles?" That perk of a championship was unavailable in 2020.

"That's something that I really wanted to get out there because, in 2020, we didn't get that parade," Roberts said later. "If there's even more incentive for winning the World Series in 2024, it's to have that parade. The way that the fans responded speaks to how passionate and how much they care about the Dodgers. It's L.A. It's about championships. I respect that." ∎

Dodgers manager Dave Roberts hoists the trophy after the Dodgers' win over the New York Mets to capture the 2024 pennant. It was the Dodgers' fourth National League title in Roberts' nine seasons as manager. (Los Angeles Daily News: Keith Birmingham)

CENTER FIELDER/SHORTSTOP

TOMMY EDMAN

The Former Cardinal Goes from Unheralded Midseason Pickup to NLCS MVP

By Jeff Fletcher | October 20, 2024

As Andrew Friedman stood on the field wearing his fresh new "National League Champions" T-shirt on Sunday night, he was asked what he expected out of Tommy Edman when he made a July trade for a guy who hadn't played all year.

"NLCS MVP," Friedman said with a smile.

The Dodgers' president of baseball operations has hit on many of his acquisitions, both big and small, throughout the team's current run of success, but his deal for Edman now looks like one of the most opportunistic.

Edman was named MVP of the NL Championship Series after hitting .407 with 11 RBIs in the six-game series, which the Dodgers wrapped up with a 10-5 victory over the New York Mets. He tied Corey Seager's Dodgers record for most RBIs in a postseason series.

"It's pretty crazy, especially with the history of the organization to have tied that record," Edman said. "I had no idea about it until I guess after the game. But a huge part of that is a testament to the guys on the team. We had really good at-bats throughout the series. Our whole lineup was really good. Any number of guys could have won MVP."

His two-run double in the first inning put the Dodgers ahead, and then his two-run homer in the third inning padded the lead.

"Unbelievable," Friedman said. "All series, he seemed to be in the middle of a lot of things we had going. Such a calm pulse. For someone who doesn't have as much postseason experience as some of our guys, he seemed to have a calmness about him that stood out."

The Dodgers acquired Edman, 29, from the St. Louis Cardinals in a three-team deal just before the July 30 trade deadline. At that point, he hadn't even played. He missed most of the season rehabbing from wrist surgery, and he hurt his ankle while working his way back.

Edman didn't play his first major league game this season until Aug. 19, three weeks after the trade.

"After the way the season started, to end up in this situation today is crazy," Edman said. "The team welcomed me with open arms. Can't wait to keep it going."

Dodgers manager Dave Roberts, who put Edman in the cleanup spot again for Game 6, said he was impressed with how much Edman was able to contribute after missing so much time.

"It's a crazy trajectory," Roberts said. "I can't say enough about the front office being able to acquire him at the deadline. You know what he can do for us on the field and (in) the clubhouse. It's just amazing. I never imagined, once we acquired him, he'd hit fourth in a postseason game. But I trust him. The guys trust him.

Tommy Edman was acquired by the Dodgers from the St. Louis Cardinals in July despite not having played a game for the Cardinals in 2024 due to injuries. (Los Angeles Daily News: David Crane)

He's made huge defensive plays for us and had huge hits. So I just very, very fortunate to have a player like Tommy."

Friedman said the Dodgers had been trying to get Edman for years. His versatility was particularly attractive.

"Just a really good baseball player," Friedman said. "(Shortstop Miguel) Rojas gets hurt and (Edman) goes from center field to shortstop. There aren't a lot of guys on Earth who can do it at such a high level. He's a really good baseball player. Just had his nose in the middle of everything we had going in the middle of the series."

Earlier in the series, Edman suggested that his initial weeks with the Dodgers amounted to spring training. He said he finally started to feel comfortable at the plate with some work he did in the break between the end of the regular season and the Division Series against the San Diego Padres.

A switch-hitter, Edman has been deadly against left-handed pitchers. He was 7 for 12 in the NLCS against lefties, including his two big hits early in Game 6 against Mets lefty Sean Manaea.

The Dodgers trailed, 1-0, in the first when Edman reached for a sweeper over the outer half and yanked it into the left field corner, for a two-run double. That accounted for the only lead change in the entire six-game series.

Two innings later, Edman got a fastball from Manaea at the top of the zone and he hit over the fence in center, a two-run homer to put the Dodgers up, 4-1.

The lead remained at least three runs for the rest of the game, sending the Dodgers into the World Series. Edman has played in the postseason with the Cardinals, but never reached the World Series.

"It's what you always dream about as a little kid, getting to play in the World Series," he said. "Playing for the Dodgers against the Yankees. It's pretty surreal. And I'm just excited to get to play those big games. We're enjoying this series win tonight. Over this next week or so we're going to start preparing against the Yankees. But it's a dream come true, for sure." ∎

Tommy Edman was named MVP of the National League Championship Series after hitting .407 with 11 RBIs in six games against the Mets. (Los Angeles Daily News: Keith Birmingham)

SOUTHERN CALIFORNIA
NEWS GROUP

Los Angeles Daily News
dailynews.com

THE ORANGE COUNTY
REGISTER
ocregister.com

PRESS-TELEGRAM
presstelegram.com

DAILY BREEZE
dailybreeze.com

THE PRESS-ENTERPRISE
pe.com

Pasadena Star-News
pasadenastarnews.com

**INLAND VALLEY
DAILY BULLETIN**
dailybulletin.com

THE SUN
sbsun.com

Redlands Daily Facts
redlandsdailyfacts.com

SAN GABRIEL VALLEY TRIBUNE
sgvtribune.com

Whittier Daily News
whittierdailynews.com

Local Brand Leaders — Known and Trusted for Over 100 Years

As premium local content providers, each of the SCNG newspapers has a long history of editorial excellence in their own respective markets — forming a special kind of trust and brand loyalty that readers really value. Exclusive local content sets the Southern California News Group apart, providing readers and users with news and information they won't find anywhere else. From local elections to their home team's top scores, when area residents need late-breaking news, SCNG newspapers, websites and mobile media are their number one resource.